Your First

100 DAYS

In a New Executive Job

Powerful First Steps on the Path to Greatness

Your First

100 DAYS

In a New Executive Job

ROBERT HARGROVE

Masterful Coaching Press, Inc
Boston, MA

Also by Robert Hargrove:

Masterful Coaching 3rd Edition

Masterful Coaching Fieldbook

Mastering the Art of Creative Collaboration

Your Coach In A Book

E-Leadership: Leadership in a Connected Age

The Great Wheel of Sales Success (ebook)

Published in the United States by

Masterful Coaching Press, Boston, MA

Library of Congress Cataloging-in-Piblication Data

Hargrove, Robert:

Your First 100 Days in a New Executive Job:

Powerful First Steps on the Path to Greatness

ISBN-1453736727

EAN-13 9781453736722

First Edition

This book is dedicated to

leaders who want to realize

an Impossible Future

and make a difference in our world.

Your First 100 Days in a New Executive Job
Powerful First Steps on the Path to Greatness

PREFACE:

How This Book is Different

For Leaders Who Want to Be Great Versus Merely Good

Whether you are president of your nation, CEO of your corporation, or a leader on the front lines, *Your First 100 Days* will show you how to take powerful first steps on the path to greatness. Every new job, however profound in scope or mundane it may seem at first glance, presents the leader with a choice: to seek an Impossible Future that alters the course of history or to just deliver on the job description. Every first 100 days requires that the leader take stock of the current situation—a group's struggles, a company's fallen fortunes, or humanity's throbbing needs and wants—and dare to take the stand that a difference can be made. Every day presents the new leader with a complex tangle of situations where they may have to offer an inspiring vision, stand up for empowering values in the face of darkness, or take bold and unreasonable action.

Seal Your Leadership With a Few Well-Chosen Words and Small Symbolic Acts

The first 100 days are on one level a time for successful executive on-boarding in a new job that looks as tough as climbing Mt Everest, shrouded in the fog of political wars and in a culture that is strange, weird, and unfamiliar. Yet on another level, it is the time when a few chosen words and symbolic acts can create a lasting impression of who you intend to be in the matter, convey what you stand for, and inaugurate a new era for your nation, company, or group. When in his inaugural address John F. Kennedy said, "The torch has been passed to a new generation of Americans," and then challenged the nation to "ask not what your country can do for you, but what you can do for your country," he instantly lifted millions of people to become their better selves.

Realize an Impossible Future that Makes a Difference While Keeping Your Day Job by Meeting Expectations

When Steve Jobs started Apple and said he was going to "change the world with the personal computer," he took a stand for an Impossible Future and inaugurated a new era. Yet at the same time, he had to deliver on his Day Job which included hiving off a project to build the Macintosh computer, making a marketing splash at the 1984 Super Bowl, setting up sales and distribution channels, returning profits to shareholders. When Indra Nooyi became CEO of Pepsi Co, one of her first priorities was to take a trip to India. She told people there that "this is a company with a soul," then said what Pepsi would do to improve drinking water and the environment.[1] The media shared this, and soda sales increased. This book is all about how to create an Impossible Future, while at the same time, delivering on your Day Job and meeting expectations.

Getting to the Top is Not Enough; You Must Master the Political Chessboard

Today presidents, CEOs, and other leaders discover in their first 100 days that, while they may have the charisma and style to land the big job, it is actually tremendously difficult for them to knit all the forces of the organization together to make something happen. Where the new leader may enter the path to greatness with a vision or goals with transformational potential, these can only be realized if the leader also finds the path to power. The book will show you how to use your first 100 days to begin to understand and master the vagaries of the political chessboard with its conflicting interests and shifting power grids. You must start, right now, immediately, to create a network of commitment, communication, and support that will allow you to move your agenda forward.

Inspiration to Reach for the Stars and a Treasure Trove of Practical Advice to Apply Immediately

What makes this book different is the powerful context it is wrapped in, much more than any tip or technique. This context is largely defined by such distinctions as: *"path to greatness"* versus *"path to power,"* *transformational* versus *transactional* leadership, *create an Impossible Future* versus *deliver on your Day Job, mastering the political chessboard* (playing their game) versus *being a change insurgent* (play your game). *Your First 100 Days* provides successful winning strategies and practical advice: start with your going-in mandate; assess current reality; create a 100 Day Plan; turn things around; define the opportunity; realign the organization; get some quick wins; and manage your boss. Yet it takes into account that these tools will not get you all the way to the top of the mountain, they really only represent the necessary equipment to have in your pack as you set out from the base camp.

Discover How to Call Yourself Forth into Your New Job Situation

Make your job a transformational assignment. Every job is what you make of it and an opportunity to remake yourself in the process. You can choose to live out your job description or to go for a big vision that will require reinventing the organization, recognizing that you may have to reinvent yourself first. This book will help you break the grip and excel beyond the "winning strategies" that got you here, but which may not get you there. You will be encouraged to take a look at your job and ask, *"Who do I need to be and what do I need to do in order to succeed?"* It will teach you how to call yourself forth into the emerging situation as needed—for example, as a tough boss or servant leader, visionary game-changer or inspired profit mechanic, cop or coach.

Taken as a whole, your first 100 days in your new leadership role can be the ultimate self-development and growth experience.

INTRODUCTION:

Don't Just Hit the Ground Running But Sprinting as the Clock is Ticking From Day One

CONGRATULATIONS! YOU'VE WON. You have begun your first 100 days in a big, new job, one that comes with high expectations and demands that you perform from day one. You may be a new leader of your nation in a crisis, the CEO of a big corporation in an economic downturn, the director of a school or hospital that needs reinvention, someone on the front lines of your business, or in the government or the military. You may feel yourself alternating between *euphoria* that this could be just the opportunity to realize an Impossible Future and make a difference you've been waiting for and *fatigue* due to the staggering demands of your Day Job.

As executive search consultants Thomas Neff and James Citrin provocatively ask, *"So you're in charge! Now what?²"* *What do you think about and do first to have a successful onboarding experience? How do you seal your leadership and make your mark? Do you have the right people on the bus? How do you make sure you get enough coaching on the vagaries of the political chessboard and culture to make sure you don't bump your head on the transparent Plexiglas door on your way into the board room or bosses office? How do you avoid costly mistakes?*

Your First 100 Days is a Time to Not Only Hit the Ground Running, *But Sprinting*

> *The First 100 Days is not just about*
> *executive onboarding, but about sealing*
> *your leadership and making your mark.*

According to one CEO, "The words climbing Mt. Everest, steep learning curve, and disaster management quickly spring to mind when I look back on my first 100 days." "The sheer avalanche of email, phone calls, meetings and workload that hurtles towards you is staggering," said a newly-elected MP in Britain. "I had a mandate, but I don't think anything can prepare you for the roller coaster ride of trying to actually bring about change," said a business unit manager. One thing is certain, the first 100 days is a time to shape events before they shape you. It is a time to sound the tone that you want to be a *great* leader, not just a *good* one. It's a time to figure out the conflicting demands of your vision and Day Job. It's a time to gather and distill information. It's a time to take your change agenda and get at least a piece of it over the line before the window of opportunity closes.

Your First 100 Days Will Be Viewed as a Measure of Your Leadership Dynamism

The idea of the "first 100 days" was given birth by Franklin Delano Roosevelt (FDR) as a measure of leadership dynamism and has become the benchmark for assessing the early successes of United States presidents. FDR, who took office in 1933 in the midst of the Great Depression, realized that there was no honeymoon period and he used his first 100 days to hit the ground running. FDR chose to forego the traditional celebratory balls on the eve of his Inauguration and instead used that time to hand-craft a 100 Day Plan. Also it was that same day, in an unprecedented fashion that his cabinet was unceremoniously sworn in at the White House. Almost immediately there was a change in Washington. FDR pushed 15 major bills through Congress in his first 100 days and has since come to personify the term "first 100 days". "I do not see how any living soul can last physically going the pace that he is going," said Senator Hiram Johnson of FDR at the time, "and mentally any one of us would be a psychopathic case, if we undertook to do what he is doing."[3]

Your First 100 Days Will Be Viewed as a Bellwether of Your Leadership Effectiveness

Whether you are a newly installed head of state, business executive, or military officer, you are likely to have to start your first 100 days on a very steep and slippery slope. How well you deal with the climb will be viewed as a benchmark of your leadership effectiveness. When Barack Obama became President, he was immediately faced with a global financial meltdown that posed the collapse of the American banking system. He didn't have a simple answer or obvious plan, but he did take dramatic steps to get the economy back on track. When General David Petraeus took over command of Afghanistan after General Stanley McChrystal was fired, his first task was to convince the American people that we had gained enough momentum to win the war, rather than just plan for a graceful exit. When Jeff Immelt became CEO of General Electric, he was asked, "How many days do you think you have to make your mark?" He said, "None! You are expected to perform from day one." [4]

The leader's first job is to define
reality. -Max Dupree

Have a Story Ready as Stakeholders Will Look for Important Signals Immediately

Whether you are taking over the leadership of a super successful organization or one that has been knocked back on its heels in a brawl with the competition, stakeholders will be watching and waiting to hear what kind of mark you intend to make. When Jack Welch took over as CEO of General Electric, it was already a successful company. He held a press conference at the Pierre Hotel in New York City in which he was asked about this vision. He said that GE would be #1 or #2 in every business it was in. When Tim Armstrong took over as CEO of AOL after its separation from Time Warner, people asked whether the company had a future. Armstrong said AOL was a great brand with strong assets. He added that although it was a content site, AOL had a new breakthrough technology that would make it a key player in social networking. The point is, get your story ready from day one, as stakeholders will look for important signals immediately. Make it be a transformation story, shift from something old to something new.

People are afraid of change, but want change.

One of the First Jobs of a New Leader is to Get People to Face Reality

It's my observation that when a new leader comes into a job and does their due diligence, they often discover that the people in their organization have been shading or avoiding reality with regard to the difficult facts and circumstances their organization is facing. *How can we be so blind to the fact that the people who elected us are turned off by our party's indifference to the issue of affordable healthcare and will vote us out of office if we don't act? How can we not recognize that airline customers are deeply frustrated not just with our company, but the entire industry? How come we act as if we don't know that costs are spinning completely out of control?* One of the first jobs a leader will need to do is to bring his or her team together and get people to face reality. In many cases, this paradoxically leads to a discussion of a vision of what's really possible.

It is Better to Be Known for Shock and Awe vs. Walking on Egg Shells

On 11 May, 2010, David Cameron succeeded Gordon Brown as Prime Minister of Great Britain, taking the helm of the country's first coalition government since 1945. At the age of 43, Cameron was the youngest British leader since Lord Liverpool in 1812. Cameron took advantage of the combination of a brief honeymoon period and his mandate from the voters who wanted change. The May 2010 Queen's Speech which marks the commencement of Parliament proposed a program of radical government for radical change, "one that will affect our economy, our society – indeed, our whole way of life." The Queen's Speech (on Cameron's and the coalition government's behalf) unveiled 23 bills and one draft bill detailing ambitious plans for major reform of schools, welfare, the police, and the political system. On August 18th, 2010, Cameron marked his first 100 days in office. His style as Prime Minister during this time had been the same style that secured him the conservative party head, one of shock and awe.[5] In contrast, liberal Gordon Brown had walked on eggshells in his first 100 days and has since been viewed as being weak.

Even Without a Proper Mandate, You Can Bring About Intended Change By Building Coalitions

Leaders like FDR and Barack Obama had a mandate to bring about change by virtue of winning the election. In David Cameron's case, he didn't even win, but merely became Prime Minister as a result of building a coalition government with the support of liberal Democrat Nick Clegg. Inside the space of two months and behind the cover of an "emergency" and "unavoidable" budget, Cameron took steps to dismantle the British Welfare State that was bankrupting the country. It wasn't long before Cameron began to get push back from the opposition: "Unless the policy is reversed, it will wreck the coalition, increase social conflict, and damage the country."[6] Nonetheless, Cameron was able to get enough of his change agenda through Parliament in his first 100 days so as to be able solidify his political position and build momentum.

Your First 100 Days Requires Situational Leadership

This book is written for both government and business leaders, which requires that at times you may need to read the book extrapolatively. If I use a business example, you need to extrapolate that to government and vice a versa. Having said that, I think business leaders will find the STARS Model—which shows the different phases of business evolution—very useful in both assessing their situation and developing a strategy to match. Ask yourself which situation you are walking into and then reflect on the strategies that are suggested next to them.

DIAGRAM I.I THE STARS MODEL OF BUSINESS EVOLUTION TO ASSESS
YOUR SITUATION AND THEN FIND A CORRESPONDING STRATEGY TO
MATCH.

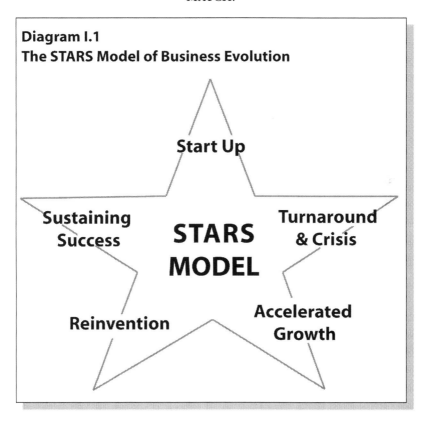

Diagram I.1
The STARS Model of Business Evolution

Start Up

Sustaining
Success

**STARS
MODEL**

Turnaround
& Crisis

Reinvention

Accelerated
Growth

ARE YOU IN A START UP SITUATION?

Situation: The business was started with a "great idea" and hard work. The problem is not enough staff, customers, or cash.

Strategy: You need to make sure you are targeting a high growth market. Develop a brand value proposition, provide exceptional value to customers and become a sales hound.

ARE YOU IN A TURNAROUND OR CRISIS SITUATION?

Situation: Here the business model seems to have run out of gas with problems with operations and customers and staff defecting. The business is losing money and you need to do something urgently.

Strategy: Come into the job and have a story ready day one that will give confidence to key employees, customers, and other stakeholders. Stabilize the situation with a 100-day turnaround plan that starts with getting everyone to face reality. Make some tough people decisions and do something to stop the bleeding.

ARE YOU IN AN ACCLERATED GROWTH SITUATION?

Situation: The company has weathered the start-up and turnaround or crisis stage, and is now in accelerating growth. While there is a good growth strategy, there are not enough good leaders to carry it out. The products and services are good, but many business processes are either missing or dysfunctional.

Strategy: Don't think in terms of doing it all yourself, but focus on creating a team of 'A' players. Your mindset: "get me the best in the world," rather than just fill slots. Do an assessment on what's working and not working, and address what's missing that could make a difference— *build a brand name, leverage new technology, and outsource missing or broken processes.*

ARE YOU IN A REINVENTION SITUATION?

Situation: The company has achieved a degree of critical mass and is being pushed along by the momentum of the marketplace. However, the innovative product or service that helped it to grow into a Global 1000 is being commoditized, and sales and margins are shrinking. Profits are maintained through cost cuts. Employees are setting reasonable goals and pursuing incremental improvement. Meanwhile, the Chinese are already in your market and eating your lunch.

Strategy: Start by praising the team for taking the organization to the top of the mountain, but declare that it is time to climb the next peak. Bring people together and present a white paper that shows how the industry is changing due to globalization, new competitor's fresh from the niche, or new technology, and that you must change too. Brainstorm a game-changing strategy, product, or service. Launch with a 100 day catalytic breakthrough project. Design one to three change initiatives that will reinvent core business processes. Put out TPOV to shift culture from creeping incrementalism and entitlement to one of breakthrough and accountability.

ARE YOU IN A SUSTAINING SUCCESS SITUATION?

Situation: Rather than an entrepreneur who creates something new, this company has been run by a steward who upholds what made the organization successful. Think of the CEO of a company like Boeing, the Chancellor of Harvard University, and the President of Switzerland. These organizations work, but a loss of vision or slip up in values can seriously tarnish the organization's image or lead to more serious problems.

Strategy: Provide a vision of the future and keep advancing the state of the art of the product, while continuing to uphold the governing values that made the organization great. Always act like you are on stage in terms of your personal behavior, because you are. Boeing was a successful company for generations, but its business success and credibility was seriously harmed by its CEO's ethical violations.

Focus Your First 100 Days Not Just on What Ultimately Should Be Done, but What *Can* Be Done

Although FDR was elected in 1932 by a majority, it was not a landslide. He knew that, while he had a mandate to end the Great Depression, it was limited by the opposition of both Hoover Republicans and Huey Long Populists. FDR didn't know exactly what to do to deliver on his campaign promise to "put a chicken in every pot," so he asked questions and listened. He decided to "focus not on what *could* be done, but rather what *can* be done." He proved himself to be an able *transactional* leader in his first 100 days, wheeling and dealing in Congress to pass a torrent of legislation of remedial make-work programs.

"In the 100 days from March to June [1933]," wrote the American journalist Walter Lippmann, in the wake of FDR's first 100 day reforms, "we became again an organized nation, confident of our power to provide for our own security and to control our own destiny."[7] It wasn't until FDR's second 100 days, after he put together the great electoral coalition of 1936, that he became a *transformational* leader and passed legislation that amounted to an economic Bill of Rights for all Americans. In the words of the historian Arthur Schlesinger, his first 100 days were "the start of a process that ended by transforming American society."[8]

> *The clock is ticking from day one. You have 100 days to prove yourself or you will be out the door. -Daniel Vasella, CEO, Novartis*

A CEO or Team Leader? In Business or Government? Most 100 Days Issues Are the Same

Jim Burns, author of the Franklin Delano Roosevelt biography, *The Lion and the Fox,* told me a story about his days in World War II that helps to illustrate the notion that new leaders often face the same issues whatever level they are on. "I was assigned, not just to combat but to be an army historian. I noticed once the fighting started, the colonels, captains, and lieutenants dropped into the background and leadership became the task of first lieutenants and sergeants." The new Commanding Office would have a short time to: 1) Get clear on their mission, "Here are our orders," 2) Establish his leadership through immediate decisions and actions; 3) Get clear on the problem the group is facing; 4) Set goals and priorities and mobilize people; 5) Demonstrate (teach) the right attitudes; and 6) Defeat the enemy on the battle field and win the population.[9]

Act Like You Are on Stage at All Times, Because You Are

When Nelson Mandela stepped up to the podium for his Inaugural speech as President of South Africa, he made a stirring speech in which one of the themes was compassion for those who had been part of the Apartheid regime. Yet, what electrified the nation was that sitting next to him were his jailers from Robyn Island. Mandela, knowing he was on stage, skillfully orchestrated their appearance to make his point. Your first 100 days is a time when small steps or missteps—things spoken or misspoken—can have long-range consequences.

Bill Clinton's stand for "gays in the military" in his first week in office is a classic example of this, one that cost him dearly. James McNerney of Boeing spend part of his first 100 days deciding whether or not to pay a $600 million fine levied on the company for ethical violations by his predecessors. He decided to pay it to establish that Boeing was an ethical company, and the badly shaken morale of employees rebounded.

The START MODEL Provides a Sure-Fire 100-Day Template for Getting Off to a Flying Start

Here is a simple template for getting off to a flying start in your first 100 days. Any new leader, whether the head of a nation, the CEO of a company, or a front-line leader, can practically and immediately apply this template. While studying new leaders who have been successful in their first 100 days, I have noticed that their approach almost invariably follows a certain pattern. I have articulated this pattern here so as to give you a mental model for how to approach your first 100 days. I call it the START Model. The START model is different from the STARS model we previously mentioned. This model is the underlying "red thread" that knits many of the chapters in this book together.

Diagram I.2 START Model
A Template for Your First 100 Days

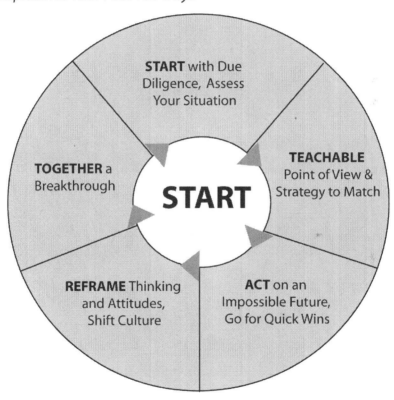

START with Due Diligence, Assess Your Situation

TEACHABLE Point of View & Strategy to Match

TOGETHER a Breakthrough

START

REFRAME Thinking and Attitudes, Shift Culture

ACT on an Impossible Future, Go for Quick Wins

The START MODEL is a powerful, concise template that tells you exactly what you need to do in your first 100 days

1. Start with due diligence, assess your situation

What's your going in mandate? For government leaders: *Why were you elected? Why did they throw the others out?* For business leaders: *What is the difference you are expected to make? What is the Day Job you need to perform?* Conduct due diligence interviews. *What is the problem? What needs to change?* Business leaders use the STARS Model to assess your situation: *1) Start Up, 2) Turnaround, 3) Accelerated Growth, 4) Reinvention, 5) Sustain Success.*

2. Teachable point of view and strategy to match the situation

Develop a "teachable point of view" (TPOV) about success: *This is who I am and what I stand for as a leader*, and use that to introduce yourself to the organization. Develop a strategy to match the situation. For example, *Deal proactively with turnaround or crisis and take action within 72 hours*. Set goals and priorities for first 100 days with the intent of having an impact. Get your team to face reality. Make unreasonable requests.

3. Act on an Impossible Future and go for quick wins

Declare an Impossible Future and start building a shared vision at town hall meetings. Get going and create a *virtuous* circle of increasing credibility through a succession of quick wins, rather than a *vicious* circle of decreasing credibility through elaborate planning and preparation.

4. Re-frame thinking and attitudes, shift culture

Further develop your "teachable point of view" about success in your government or business that tells people, "This is how we are going to win." For example for government leaders, a TPOV might be "All lives have equal value." For business leaders, it might be: "Drive revenue growth and profit growth through innovation." Put out your TPOV with every breath you take.

5. Together, a Breakthrough!

Make everyone a player in the "big game" by getting them to set leadership and business challenges in alignment with the Impossible Future. Ask each person on your staff to create an impossible goal every 90 days. Turn these into a "catalytic breakthrough project" that will take you and your organization to a different place.

This Book is Intended to Inspire, Empower, and Enable You in Your First 100 Days

Your first 100 days is an exciting time where you have great possibilities and opportunities in front of you. But as the hexagram in the Chinese book the *I Ching* says, there is often "difficulty in the beginning." The first 100 days can result in your formulating an inspiring vision that causes everyone to say, "This is what we have all been waiting for," or it can result in costly errors in mastering the political chessboard that leave you waking up every day staring at a wall. This book has been written to inspire, empower, and enable you in the face of all of that.

Please let me know how your first 100 days goes. You can contact me at: *Robert.Hargrove@RHargrove.com*

CHAPTER 1

PREPARE YOURSELF FOR THE JOURNEY BEFORE IT STARTS

Do Your Due Diligence—Like Sherlock Holmes, Find a Watson to Discuss It With

ON MAY 23, 1492, the King and Queen of Spain issued a mandate that Christopher Columbus be authorized to find a faster trade route to the East. He was to be given three vessels—the Nina, Pinta, and Santa María—each about 50 feet long. Columbus had 25 days to make all the necessary preparations before leaving. He spent day and night studying the diaries of other explorers to glean any clues he could about navigation and to make sure that his three ships were fitted with all of the necessities.

During this preparation time, the biggest obstacle Columbus had to overcome was finding a capable crew who would enlist. At that time in history, it was believed the world was flat, and many feared the danger of getting caught in a flow of water and sailing right off the edge of the world into an endless abyss. It was believed that sea monsters, many times the size of the ships, would be waiting for them. On top of that, there were no maps to follow. To recruit a crew, Columbus walked into inns and taverns frequented by sailors and enticed them with tales of the fabulous adventures and the beautiful paradise that awaited them, of the gold-roofed palaces, of the beautiful jewel-bedecked women of the Orient and the fame that they would receive.

> *By prevailing over all distractions and*
> *obstacles, one may unfailingly arrive*
> *at his chosen dream or destination.*
> *-Christopher Columbus*

Columbus never actually achieved his original mission, yet he discovered lands he called the "Indies" that would vastly expand the known world. It was Columbus's quest for an Impossible Future — combined with the preparation period where he strengthened himself for the journey, brushed up on his navigation, and recruited his crew — that allowed him to turn bad luck into opportunity. Once Columbus eventually faced the fact that his westward journey would never lead to a faster trade route to the East, he returned to Spain and reported to King Ferdinand and Queen Isabella that, while he had met defeat on his original charter, contained within his quest was the possibility of a great triumph. This story clearly illustrates the adage: Preparation + Opportunity = Luck.

PREPARE AS IF YOU ARE STARTING OFF ON A GREAT QUEST

> *To be prepared is half the victory.*
> *-Miguel De Cervantes*

Imagine yourself like Christopher Columbus, having just been given a charter by the King and Queen to ready your ships and take off on an exciting journey. Perhaps the most pivotal piece of advice is to take the time (30 days if possible) to prepare for the journey rather than just show up in time to take the helm. Imagine setting off to circumnavigate the globe in a small sailboat, to climb Mt. Everest, or to explore Antarctica without first taking the time to make thorough preparations.

One thing is certain: the bigger the job you are undertaking, the more preparation time you will need. Every new President of the United States has the time between his election in November and the inauguration in January to prepare for the job. This period of time is traditionally used to get a clearer understanding of your vision, goals, and change agenda, as well to begin mastering the political chessboard. It is also the time to get the best and brightest people on the bus.

Military leaders about to be assigned to a big job are often given a preparation period. I remember talking to an Army Colonel on a plane to Tokyo who was just about to be installed as the new commanding officer of the Apache Helicopter Division in South Korea. He struck me as very confident, and I asked him why. He told me he had been thinking about this job for a year. There was a slight glitch in his plans, however. Like many new leaders he had to get a handle on how to deal with an immediate crisis. This one involved the sinking of the South Korean destroyer, Cheonan, by the North Koreans.

CEOs and other business leaders, by contrast, are often thrown into the job with little or no time to prepare. James McNerney, for example, left Home Depot and went off to become CEO of 3M at the board's urgent request, with no other preparation period than a late night, three-hour plane ride to Minneapolis. He was out of the company a year later, in part because he had tried to apply GE corporate disciplines to the free-wheeling 3M culture. If ever you find yourself in a similar situation as McNerney, with people clamoring for you to show up and get started, I strongly suggest that you defer. Tell them you need a 30-day preparation period.

The Countdown Period: How to Use It Wisely

> *Confidence is preparation. Everything else*
> *is beyond your control. - Richard Kline*

Thomas J. Neff and James M. Citrin, two top-executive recruiters and authors of the book, *You're In Charge—Now What?* refer to this preparation time as the countdown period before the rocket takes off.[10] The way you approach this period will vary according to whether you come into your position from outside the organization with little advanced knowledge of the situation—or you come to the position from within the organization. It will also vary according to whether your organization is flying high or in a state of crisis.

Tony Zinni, four-star General and former combatant commander, says the countdown period is a good time to reflect on your personal philosophy of leadership, whether that be leader as visionary, leader as servant, or leader as coach. It's a good time to write down the "teachable points of view" (guiding principles) about how to win in this business or in business in general. For example: *"Every business is a growth business." "Good ideas can come from anywhere." "Spend the company's money like it's your own money."* Your first 100 days will provide you many teachable moments to interact with people in such a way as to shape thinking and attitudes and also build the culture you want.

This is the time to think not only about a vision of an Impossible Future, but also about how you will get the job done on a day-in, day-out basis. It is a time to develop a point of view about the future of your business, as well as to take account of the current and past performance of your organization. It is a time to ask questions that will allow you to learn as much as possible about the challenges your organization is facing, while both distilling valuable information about the solution and also questioning biases.

Simultaneously, you will need to prepare yourself physically and emotionally for a major life transition. One CEO told me that on the day he was appointed to the job, "I changed some of my eating habits and started working out 7 days a week. By the time my first 100 days period was over, I had peeled off over 30 pounds and I was down to my college weight." He was full of vim and vigor and ready to deal with the immense task in front of him.

It is also important to get your family and support infrastructure ready to run without you for a period of time. This is going to be a time of total dedication, and your family needs to understand this. At the same time, you need to consciously set aside time for your spouse and create perhaps even a "date night" with each one of your children as you go forward.

You should approach this entire preparation period as the beginning of a strategic process that culminates in coming up with at least a rough draft of your 100-Day Plan. Dan Schulman, CEO of Virgin Mobile USA, says "The days leading up to your first one hundred days are some of the most important for your success. Day one on the job had better not be day one where you are putting your action plan in place. Your action plan should be well underway by the time you get there."[11]

STUDY UP ON THE ORGANIZATION—DUE DILIGENCE

> *There is a way of enquiring, of engaging*
> *in questions that is actually empowering*
> *with respect to the questioner.*

During the countdown period it is very important to study up on the organization and the task in front of you, as you will probably have a limited time in which to do this once the job actually starts.

To be sure, there will be a lot of reading for you to do, documents such as government or think-tank White Papers, the corporation's annual report, balance sheets, or Form 10Ks. You can also learn a lot by looking up your company on Google or other internet sources. It is important to frame your line of inquiry by asking questions and listening loudly.

As a new leader, you probably already have many questions emerging from your mind about the job, the organization, and the task in front of you. It is better to engage and enquire, adopting a basic attitude of learning, curiosity, and humility, than it is to adopt the attitude of knowing, certainty, and management hubris. There is a way of enquiring, of engaging in questions that is very empowering with respect to the questioner. It involves choosing a handful of questions to ask, and then living inside each question until you go beyond answers and come to moments of true insight.

IF YOU ARE THE PRESIDENT OF A COUNTRY, DEPARTMENT HEAD, OR ELECTED OFFICIAL YOU MIGHT ASK:

- *What mandate was I given by the people who elected (appointed) me?*
- *What problems am I supposed to solve?*
- *How am I supposed to solve them?*

FDR came into the presidency during the Great Depression. When he got to the White House he really didn't have any answers. So he began meeting with people morning, noon, and night, even while taking a bath, to get their views on the problem, as well as getting to fundamental causes and solutions.

IF YOU ARE A NEW CORPORATE CEO OR EXECUTIVE, INQUIRE INTO THESE ISSUES:

- *What is this company's greatest strategic opportunity?*
- *What is its present and past performance operationally?*
- *What can be done to run the business better?*
- *Do we have the right people on the bus?*

You will start this line of investigation during the countdown period, but you may continue it after your start day when you have more access to people and information. Remember, it's not only about what questions you choose, but also about developing an ability to live inside those questions until you start to have eye-opening insights and get to the "aha" moment.

Conduct Due Diligence Interviews with the Passion of Sherlock Holmes on an Investigation

It is important in the due diligence process not to get blindsided by your own pre-conceptions or the point of view of people inside the company. In coaching all of my executive clients at the outset of a new job, I use a method which I call the *Due Diligence Interviews.* The Due Diligence Interviews are all about coming up with a list of fascinating and intriguing people with different views and perspectives and then engaging with them in questions. This is a good technique for coming up to speed on the situation you are walking into and then defining both your Impossible Future and your Day Job goals.

The kind of questions you ask might vary if you are for example president of a country, CEO of a company, or director of a hospital, but they echo common themes.

- *What throbbing human needs and wants do the people of this state or district have, and what can we do, despite our limited resources, to help?*
- *As a customer, what's your point of view about this company?*
- *How are we to work together as business partners?*
- *What has this organization accomplished in recent years that is new and noteworthy, and have we communicated it well?*
- *What do you see as possible and achievable?*
- *How would you define the biggest problem in one sentence?*
- *What do you see as the biggest opportunity in front of us?*
- *If you were in my job, what would you do?*
- *What's missing from this picture?*
- *What changes would you suggest?*

To give you the right mindset for engaging people in dialogue during these interviews, I want to introduce you to a three-step process we use in our program called the *CollabLab—an Accelerated Solutions Event*. The process consists of three phases: 1) Scan, 2) Focus, and 3) Act[12]. (See Diagram 1.1)

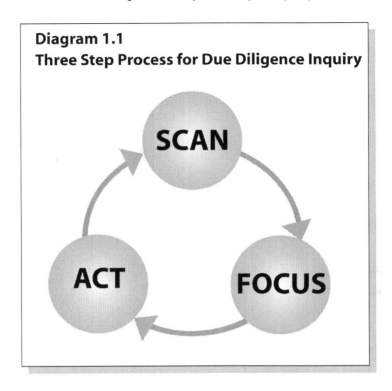

Diagram 1.1
Three Step Process for Due Diligence Inquiry

In Scan, you scan the horizon to gather as many different views and perspectives as possible on the questions at hand about the organization. For example, to help a new leader or team accelerate their learning curve, we often use something called the "What's So" process where we ask: *What has been accomplished? What is the problem (fact-based)? What are the strategic opportunities? What's missing that will allow you to solve the problem or seize the opportunities?* In Focus, you sort out all the opinions you have gathered and start to come to conclusions. In Act, you begin to put together an initial 100 Day Plan and gear yourself to take action from day one.

The key to the success of the Due Diligence Interviews is to stay in "scan" mode long enough and with a rich enough mix of people that you not only get to the real problem, but also come up with new ideas, fresh approaches, and innovative solutions. You have to be willing to go beyond the secret handshakes of the board about what will be voted up or down, the old shared understandings of the executive committee about what's possible and achievable, as well as the standard industry orthodoxies.

DUE DILIGENCE INTERVIEW PROCESS

THE DUE DILIGENCE INTERVIEW PROCESS CONSISTS OF FOUR STEPS

I.   Come up with a list of 50 fascinating and intriguing people to interview
II. Develop a list of questions that will tell you what you need to know.
III. Engage in questions until you gain moments of true insight.
IV. Find a coach or a thinking partner to help synthesize the answers.

Let's look at each one.

I. Come Up With a List of 50 Fascinating and Intriguing People to Interview

Never waste a lunch.

I suggest that you start by creating a hotlist of 50 to 100 people to interview. I also suggest that you spend a good chunk of your preparation time and even the first month on the job passionately engaged in carrying out the interviews. If you are in the United States government for example, your list might include White House operatives, colorful people from the Department of State or Defense, people from the media with strong opinions, bright people from think-tanks, as well as colorful people from your own department, especially those who were silenced in the past.

If you are working in a corporation, your hot list could include thought-leaders from the company, competitors, customers, Wall Street types, and the national and trade press. I know this may seem like a lot, but it is well worth the time you put into it, and if you have a coach to act as a thinking partner, you can speed up the process.

One important aspect of the Due Diligence Interviews is that they allow you to make the acquaintance of new people, as well as to refresh your relationships with people you may not have talked to in years. Just pick up the phone and tell the people involved that you are interested in their opinion, and you will be surprised how many people respond with enthusiasm. A good way to do the interviews, if you have the time, is to invite people to lunch or out for a cup of coffee.

II. Develop a List of Questions That Will Tell You What You Need to Know

> *To find the right answers, start*
> *with the right questions.*

QUESTIONS TO BE ANSWERED IN THE DUE DILIGENCE INTERVIEWS

- What has been accomplished?
- What is the biggest problem?
- What is the greatest strategic opportunity?
- How do things work around here in order to bring about change?

Let's look more closely at each of these four questions:

What has been accomplished? You don't want to be the kind of leader who walks onto the scene, criticizes his predecessor, and then proceeds to make everyone and everything in the organization wrong. That is a good way to not only turn everyone off in your first 100 days, but also to demoralize your entire organization. You do want to be the kind of leader who goes around and asks people: *What has been accomplished in recent years (or months)?* Accomplishments have a way of not being adequately communicated, and as a result, they disappear into the woodwork. Asking this question is a way to not only bring accomplishments to light but also to discover sources of hidden strategic strength that can be tapped in the future. It is also a way to acknowledge people for a job well done.

One of the things that CEO Tim Armstrong discovered in his first 100 days at AOL after its separation from TimeWarner was that, whereas people did know the traditional story of AOL, they did not know the real story. Although AOL had excelled in providing internet content management in the past, in recent years they had developed technologies called Media Glow that put the company on the forefront of combining text messaging with social networking. The issue was that neither AOL's customers nor their partners knew about this.

As Armstrong said in his first 100 days memo to the entire company, "Before coming to AOL, I spoke with a lot of people about this company, and the views generally fell into two camps. The first group thought AOL and the AOL brands were past the point of no return. The second group thought AOL was a misunderstood and underestimated asset. It probably won't come as a shock that, after spending 100 days with all of you, my view falls strongly into the second camp – AOL is an incredible asset and it can be improved."[13]

What is the biggest problem? I think one of the most important things to watch out for when interviewing people is that many are in denial about the problem. For example, when Howard Stringer took over as CEO of Sony Corporation, one of the due diligence questions he asked was: *"How did Sony Corporation, the inventor of the Walkman, allow Apple to so suddenly topple Sony's dominance of the market with the iPod?"* He discovered that many in the company looked at Apple's triumph as a mere fluke and they actually denied that there was a real problem. Stringer realized that one of his first jobs as a leader was going to be to get people to face reality. He did this through a fact-based presentation and by being intentionally provocative and walking around the Sony corporate headquarters with an Apple iPod.

QUESTIONS DESIGNED TO HELP YOU TO "GET" REALITY

- Is the company growing profitably or not? If not, why not?
- Are we pretending that our brand is strong when it really is weak?
- Does our strategic positioning fit yesterday, but not today or tomorrow?
- Are members of our executive team in love with our products, while being blindfolded with respect to the terrible customer experience?
- Are we spending more money than we are making?

What is our greatest strategic opportunity? One of the things about CEOs of big companies is that they tend to be victims of old industry orthodoxies and, as such, are not open to messages the competitive environment is trying to tell them about the opportunities and threats facing their company. For example, in the 1970's during the days of the oil shocks, a group of big oil CEOs predicted that, based on the exploration and production methods of the time, the world's oil supply would run out by just about now (2010) and oil prices would sky rocket.

However, British Petroleum (BP) was smart enough to hire as its new CEO Sir John Browne, whose aggressive attitude and sense of curiosity during his first 100 days led him to interact with a small start-up at the edge of the oil industry that was experimenting with some new offshore drilling techniques. Presto! BP's potential oil reserves quadrupled almost overnight, and the rest of the industry followed suit. The world's known oil reserves have multiplied dramatically since these and other new techniques were discovered. Of course, this was before the Blue Water Horizon disaster when overly aggressive behavior led to big problems for the BP.

QUESTIONS DESIGNED TO REVEAL STRATEGIC OPPORTUNITIES

- What is the biggest issue or problem your organization (industry) is facing?
- What's happening in the environment? What's coming next?
- What possibilities are you willing to declare open?
- Where is the opening to transform that possibility to a concrete opportunity?

How do things work around here in order to bring about change? There are forces at play in a big organization and, if you understand them, it's actually possible to harness these forces. I have found that all too often, new executives, while having a vision and a game plan, will fall on their swords, because instead of figuring out how they can be a co-flow with these forces, they wind up being a cross-flow or a counter-flow.

SOME QUESTIONS TO GAIN INSIGHT INTO HOW THINGS WORK

- Are you aware of any secret handshakes between members of the executive committee that may help or hinder any new initiatives coming from my area?
- What suggestions, if any, do you have for how to get my bosses' buy-in?
- Do you recommend a big strategic planning document, or small wins?
- How does the CEO (or members of the executive committee) react to bad news?
- Has anyone you know been fired or censured for speaking their mind or discussing issues that were previously undiscussable?

Over and above the three questions in the Due Diligence Interviews, you should also include questions that are specific to your own concerns, like: *How do we build this business exponentially? How do we build a global brand? How do we improve safety?* The idea is to come up with a short but powerful list of questions that tell you what you need to know.

For example, in coaching one company's brand manager who had the mandate to make the company one of the most recognized brands in the world, we asked the following questions: *1) What do you think of when you think of our company? 2) What do you think our differentiator is? 3) What do you think our differentiator could be, given our strategic strengths and changes in the environment?* We stayed in these questions long enough that we eventually started to think outside the box and came up with a powerful and unique brand differentiator. Also, it may be helpful to gear your questions to specific functions.

QUESTIONS FOR SPECIFIC FUNCTIONS

Board Members: What are you trying to do at your board meeting? How does the group work together?

Finance: What are the idiosyncrasies of the planning and budgeting process?

Engineering: What "wow" products are in the pipeline; what are the growth engines of the future?

Marketing: What is the company's dramatic difference or key brand differentiator?

Supply Chain: Are we the lowest cost, highest quality producer? How could we be?

Human Resources: What are we doing to attract, develop, and keep rock stars of talent?

III. Engage in Questions Until You Gain Moments of True Insight

Engaging in questions can be more empowering than answers.

I recommend that you do the interviews yourself or delegate some to a coach or confidant. I would advise telling people that whatever they say will be confidential, or at least not attributable to them. Take copious notes when you ask people the questions; this seems to improve the committed speaking on other people's part and the committed listening on yours. I have found that asking people what they think, not only allows them to provide their own insights into what is happening, but also gets them involved.

IV. Find a Coach or a Thinking Partner to Help Synthesize the Answers

Elementary my dear Watson!

You may discover that by the time you have interviewed 5 to 10 people, you feel like you are drinking from a fire hose without a way to mentally digest all that you hear. Again, a coach or thinking partner will help in this regard—a Watson to your Sherlock. Have an afternoon tête-à-tête with your coach once a day to go through the interviews. This will give you a chance to step back and see the big picture and to make sense of the random ideas, observations, and insights that are coming at you, as well as to connect the dots. You could ask your coach to take notes on the key themes as you speak. This can be very useful in helping to prepare a White Paper which is a good tool for helping to create a mandate for change. Make sure you save your notes so you can go back and get exact quotes.

DUE DILIGENCE IS PIVOTAL IN SETTING GOALS AND INITIATING ACTION IN YOUR FIRST 100 DAYS

Paul Drechsler of Wates Group Ltd, a large construction company in England, emphasizes the importance of "walking your job" rather than getting trapped in one's office in those critical first 100 days. During his first 30 days, his preparation period prior to starting the job, he spoke to five stock marketing analysts, thirty customers, and fifteen business partners. When he took office on day one, he began a process that involved speaking with 700 employees to learn about their perceptions of the company.

This period of due diligence, according to Drechsler, gave him powerful insights about the company's strengths and weaknesses and specifically what needed to change. Drechsler then used his second thirty days to set goals and priorities, as well as to get feedback on the goals from people inside and outside the company who he had developed confidence in and made a relationship with during his initial Due Diligence Interviews. He asked questions like: "Are these the right goals?" and "Will they take us down the right path?"

In his third 30 days, Drechsler began making important decisions and executing with the view of making some rather dramatic changes. "The decisions you make will instantly tell people what's important to you and signal a shift in the wind."[14]

PRACTICE AND REFLECTION ASSIGNMENTS

You are about to embark on a new executive venture with both an Impossible Future and a big Day Job in your sights. You are going to have to come up with your game plan, bring your team together, and master the vagaries of the political chessboard. This kind of undertaking tends to be totally absorbing of one's time and attention. In order to be able to tackle "climbing Mount Everest," you need to be in good shape in every respect. It's important to be not only spiritually and mentally in shape, but physically in shape as well. I have created a series of Practice and Reflection assignments to do in your 30 day preparation period to help you to prepare you and your family for a period of your total commitment and involvement in your new job.

Practice and Reflection Assignment 1: Leadership Preparation

Write a one minute elevator speech that tells people in your group, "This is who I am as a leader and this is what you can expect." Take the time in the preparation period to do a brain dump on what are your leadership style and skills, the winning strategies that have made you successful in the past, and the teachable points of view that you have used to shape thinking and behavior.

Practice and Reflection Assignment 2: Will What Got You Here, Get You There?

Most leaders have a winning strategy that has made them successful. For example, Greg Goff a coachee of mine had a winning strategy of being smart, visionary, results-driven, treating everyone with respect. When Greg became CEO of a big company that was distressed, he realized he was going to have to break the grip and excel beyond his winning strategy. He was going to have to be a tougher boss than he had ever been, push for unreasonable results and make tough "people decisions".

- *Think about who you are as a leader*
- *What is the winning strategy that made you successful in your past jobs?*
- *Is your new job a big step up? Will you face issues bigger than your current self?*
- *Will your present winning strategy work in your new job?*
- *How do you need to be different? Think different? Act different?*

Practice and Reflection Assignment 3: Articulate Your TPOV for Winning

A teachable point of view (TPOV) is nothing more than a guiding principle for what it takes to be successful. TPOVs are usually honed from the great teachers we have had, books, past experiences. For example, some of my favorites TPOVs are: *"Nothing is Impossible." "Every situation is transformable." "There is always a path forward."* TPOVs can also be created in a way that helps you win in your specific business. Roberto Goizueta, former CEO of Coca Cola, put the company on a growth curve with a TPOV that changed the game from battling it out with FepsiCo over "market share" to increasing Coke's "share of stomach." Spend some time thinking about the following questions.

- *What is your personal concept of leadership as you have practiced it?*
- *Who were your great leadership role models? Boss, grandfather, coach, and so on.*
- *What is the most powerful lesson each of these people taught you (in a nutshell)? For example: "Give it your all."*
- *In your life as a professional person, what have been the defining moments?*
- *What is your TPOV about how to succeed and do you actively use it to teach others?*
- *What is the key challenge your current business or organization faces? What's a TPOV about winning in this business? (organization or nation)*

Practice and Reflection Assignment 4: Create a White Paper—The Case for Intended Change

Your Due Diligence Interviews will produce an incredible amount of information. A good practice and reflection assignment is to create a White Paper that helps to capture key insights and organize your thoughts. Creating a White Paper is also a good way to build the business case for intended change in your organization. The paper should be no more than ten pages or 30-35 PowerPoint slides, with one main point on each slide. Put the following into a White Paper or PowerPoint.

- **Accomplishments**: What is the organization's mission, what has been accomplished so far?

- **The Problem**: Express in one sentence, building a case for change
- **The Facts**: Any assessment of problems or weaknesses should be fact based
- **The Opportunity**: What's possible and achievable for this organization, given its unique strengths? What immediate opportunities are on the horizon?
- **The Strategy**: What's missing that, if provided, can make a difference?
- **Change readiness**: What can you do with existing resources and authority, now?
- **Next Steps**: Think short term catalytic breakthrough projects, or 30 day actions.

Practice and Reflection Assignment 5: Create a Rough Draft of Your First 100 Day Plan

As a new leader, you will have high expectations weighing on you in your first 100 days. It is much better to have a 100 Day Plan that focuses on goals and priorities than it is to just let the first 100 days be a random event. If you have done the White Paper, you should have plenty of ideas about what you need to accomplish in your first 100 days and beyond. It is important to have at least a rough idea of your first 100 Day Plan before you start the job. I suggest that you sketch one out on 1 to 3 pages as your first draft, then continue to iterate on a month by month basis. Check things off as you move along to motivate yourself by what you have already accomplished. In Chapter 5, we will go into further detail about the First 100 Day Plan.

- *Your Day Job description*
- *Your Impossible Future*
- *Going in mandate.*
- *3 TPOV's you have as a leader*
- *What you will accomplish in the 1st 30 days.*
- *What you will accomplish in the 2nd 30 days.*

- *What you will accomplish in the 3rd 30 days*
- *Next steps*

Practice and Reflection Assignment 6: Mental and Physical Readiness

List three leadership books that will inspire and empower you, and start to read them. For example:
- James MacGregor Burns: *Transforming Leadership*
- Doris Kearns Goodwin: *Team of Rivals*
- Jack Welch: *Winning*

Who could be a coach or mentor for your first 100 days? List three people
What are your eating habits now? How do they need to change?
What kind of exercise do you do? How do you need to adjust it? (Schedule it now.)

Practice and Reflection Assignment 7: Family Wholeness

President Truman sat down to dinner with his family every night at the White House. If someone with that kind of schedule can figure out how to make this work, why not you? Family dinners are a great way to strengthen the ties that bind. Take your attention off yourself and put it on others. Ask: "How was your day?" Get aligned on short-term family goals and priorities.

- Sit everyone in your family down and talk about how much you love them all.
- Explain that your new executive job may cause you to seem like you are less available to the family.
- Hang up a big brass bell and ask people to ring it if you seem too pre-occupied or grumpy.
- Regularly tell people in a sincere way "thank you for your understanding."

- Join your family around the supper table at least 3 to 5 times a week.
- Create a special date night for your spouse at least once a month—dinner and theatre kind of thing.
- Plan a monthly event with each child—concerts, movies and shopping. This is a good time to have fun and to talk. Never cancel!

SUMMARY

- Carve out the time to prepare—30 days before you start.
- Assess your own leadership skills and capabilities for succeeding in the job and what brought you success and how that might have to change.
- Study up on the company, starting with framing the most important questions.
- Conduct Due Diligence interviews. Understand the environment; misunderstand it at your peril!
- Make a first draft of your 100 Day Plan.
- Prepare yourself mentally, emotionally, and spiritually for a journey as steep as climbing Mt. Everest; study great leaders for insight and inspiration.
- Get into physical shape for the rigors of succeeding in your new job. You may be working long hours for the next few months.
- Tell your family you are going to be in for a rather intense ride, as you immerse yourself in your new role. Ask for their love, support, and understanding.

CHAPTER 2

GET CLEAR ON YOUR
GOING-IN MANDATE

How to Accurately Assess Your Situation and Create a Strategy to Match

IN THE SHANG Dynasty, the Emperor would give a newly appointed king or general of a region the *Mandate of Heaven*, which supported the legitimacy of that person's rule. When this king or general would first show up in the regional capital on a plumed horse with his retainers ready to take power, he would do so with the Mandate of Heaven, the full authority of the Emperor who would back him to the nines. The going-in mandate not only entrusted this person with absolute authority over the domain, but also conveyed certain marching orders – to increase open trade, suppress rebellion, and levy taxes. Unlike the Divine Right of Kings, however, the Mandate of Heaven was subject to the king's or general's conduct. Despotic rulers who quarreled with other nobles or who did not perform as expected could have their mandate withdrawn and someone would come along to take their place.

CLARIFYING EXPECTATION

> *Make sure to create a common understanding of your going-in mandate, even before you accept the position. -Jim McNerney, CEO, Boeing*

To clarify your going-in mandate, it is important to discover the answers to the certain critical questions.

CLARIFYING YOUR MANDATE IS ALL ABOUT ALIGNING EXPECTATIONS

- What are my boss's expectations of me?
- What are my expectations of my boss?
- What do my colleagues and staff expect of me?
- What do I expect of my colleagues and staff?

---

1. Do you have the boss's *Mandate of Heaven*, the legitimacy you need to shake things up? Warren Buffet may be one of the world's greatest investors, and also one of the greatest bosses. He grants the CEOs of the companies he acquires lots of power and autonomy to profitably grow the business as they choose, together with the freedom to really shake things up. He is very patient with results, even if there are billions in losses. However, when one of his CEOs does something without consulting him that destroys value (which is what happened when the CEO of Kraft

Foods sold out a highly profitable frozen pizza business in order to buy Cadbury Schweppes), he can be tough, even publically calling managers on the carpet. Where working for Warren Buffet might feel like being given the fabled *Mandate of Heaven*, many of the executives I have worked with often reach a point where they feel that they have been given the *Mandate from Hell*. The typical situation is one where the board (or CEO) hires the person to do a big job with lots of responsibility, but gives him or her little or no legitimate authority or backing to drive change in the organization.

2. **Forget what you were told. What are your real marching orders and what is the territory to be taken?** There are powerful and practical steps you can take to wind up with something closer to the Mandate of Heaven than a Mandate from Hell. This starts with engaging the CEO and others in a dialogue that helps you to precisely clarify what your real mandate is *and isn't*. There is often a maddening discrepancy between the puffed up going-in mandate that the CEO or HR described in the hiring process—"Growth is your #1 priority," "Unleash imagination and innovation," "Hire the best in the world," and so on—and the real going-in mandate that is based on the CEO's mixed feelings, frozen budgets, corporate politics, organizational culture, or initiative overload. Engaging in questions is a good way to tease out your real marching orders, and the real territory to be taken so you don't get frustrated. It is very important to know the limits of your mandate as well. When the CEO of Yahoo was asked about the company's China policies, she said, "Our mandate is to help people connect and collaborate; it is not to fix China's human rights policy. That is beyond our mandate."

3. **Are you empowered to take the bold and unreasonable actions you need in order to succeed?** Okay, you have been hired to play a key position on your team in the Great Game of Business. You want to know what is really expected of you by the CEO in terms of your role,

responsibilities, and impact. You also want to know what you can expect from the CEO and others in terms of autonomy, budget, and back up. Will you be empowered to take the bold and unreasonable actions needed to help your team win? While it is good to think positively, you don't want to deceive yourself. Now is the time to take what you thought was *implicit* when you were handed your job description and make it *explicit*. Write down the nagging questions you have about your mandate and start asking them in order to help tease out your real going-in mandate. If you feel this is too aggressive, think about your vision and game plan and start sending up some trial balloons through some experimental action. The reaction you get will tell you a lot.

QUESTIONS FOR CLARIFYING YOUR GOING-IN MANDATE

- What is my going-in mandate? Key role and responsibilities?
- What impact do I expect me to have—e.g., profitable growth?
- What needs to be changed and what is the time frame?
- What needs to be preserved? (For example: brand, quality, and so on)
- What needs to be avoided at all costs? Ethical violations?
- What am I empowered to do and not empowered to do to make it happen?
- What things can I unilaterally change without consulting my boss?
- What things should I consult my boss on before making changes?
- On what things should I let my boss make the final decision?

Clarity is Power

The more you are clear on your going-in mandate, the more powerful you will be in carrying it out. A case in point is Timothy Geithner,

USA Treasury Secretary. During his first 100 days, Geithner received a very clear mandate given the global financial crisis: "Keep America's biggest financial institutions—*JP Morgan, Citibank, Bank of America*—from going belly up and setting off what could be the next Great Depression on a global scale." Geithner's empowerment by President Obama and his clarity about his mandate enabled him to take bold and unreasonable action: 1) Bail out the banks with billions; 2) Invest in an Economic Stimulus Plan; 3) Nationalize companies like GM. The urgency of the situation demanded acting by making bold decisions and taking strong actions, without the need to look over one's shoulder. As the President said, "It's not a perfect plan," but the fact is that the economy did not flounder.

The Fog of War

In their first 100 days, most executives have to operate in a situation that is much more ambiguous than what Secretary Geithner faced. The CEO seems to solidly support you in the mandate, but there are rumors his departure is imminent. The executive community says they will crusade for your idea, but is it their actual intention to crush it? The competition is planning a big move that could change everything. Will your team rally around you or resist you? The fact is that you may find yourself trying to get clear on your going-in mandate amid what Baron Carl Von Clausewitz, the Austrian military commander referred to as "The Fog of War." Military operations depend heavily on clarity of mission, communications and situational awareness regarding the enemies' movements. When one or both of these elements becomes compromised, the result is "fog of war" which can lead to endless confusions and miscalculations in an actual combat situation. Your job is to try to take action to clear this fog or to wait it out.

STRATEGIES FOR GETTING CLEAR ON BOTH THE WHAT AND THE HOW

> *A CEO basically has to have a very powerful mandate to force change to happen, because organizations are generally like bodies in motion that tend to stay in motion.*
>
> *-John Malone, CEO, Liberty Media*

As we said, getting clear on your going-in mandate is all about aligning expectations: people's expectations of you and your expectations of others. Lack of clarity in aligning expectations can place people on different roadmaps. For example, Jim McNerney went from being a CEO candidate at GE to becoming CEO of 3M almost overnight. After one executive onboarding conversation, which consisted of a 90-minute plane flight, McNerney thought he was clear about his going-in mandate which was to grow the business and decrease costs. He knew the *what* of the mandate, but he lacked strategies to find out the *how*—just how much leeway he would have in accomplishing this was foggy.

The 3M board was okay with the idea of McNerney reeling in 3M's wildcat scientists who had previously spent gobs of money on R&D projects not tied to the market. However, they balked and fired McNerney after just a few months when he seemed to be working toward replacing 3M's culture of encouraging innovation and experimentation, by putting in GE's Six Sigma process efficiency and tight cost controls. This example shows how important it is, even for the most highly-rated CEOs, to have enough executive on-boarding conversations to both clarify the mandate and dissipate any fogginess that surrounds it. It's a good idea to spend time in dialogue, perhaps over dinner, where the boss can find out more about who you are and your approach to impacting the business and you can find out more about the boss and company and how your approach would go over.

> *Consider your going-in mandate not as handed down from on high, but as the act of co-creating something through the process of dialogue.*

Stretch Your Mandate for an Impossible Dream Through Dialogue

The chances are that when the CEO discussed your going-in mandate, like "grow the business", "cut costs", "or win the talent war," the conversation was a one-way monologue. That is okay for starters, but now that you know more about the real situation, you may need to stretch your mandate, which requires engaging the CEO in a dialogue. "Since I took this job, my goals have moved into kind of an impossible dream, and I may have to do things that are radical, just to accomplish my Day Job." By definition, authentic dialogue is never superficial chit–chat; it is always a shared inquiry in which participants share different views and perspectives and seek to build shared understanding about mutual concerns. I have observed that whenever a real quality of dialogue is reached, people are bonded to each other in ways that make for a great working relationship going forward.

RULES FOR DIALOGUE

- Treat everyone as a colleague
- Conduct a shared inquiry into mutual concerns
- It's okay to disagree
- Build shared understanding that leads to something new
- Discuss the undiscussable

Lifting the Fog: Authentic Communication vs. Superficial Congeniality

I have observed that the process of getting clear on the going-in mandate involves lifting the fog of war that obscures it. Yet how do you deal with fog-creating factors like the CEO's mixed messages, competing political agendas on the executive committee, competition for talent and resources and, for lack of a better word, BS communication where people say one thing and think another? It is my belief that if there is one thing a leader can do to bring some brilliant sunshine into what is probably a very murky situation, and that is committed speaking and listening.

PERPLEXED ABOUT YOUR JOB MANDATE? WHICH FOG OF WAR FACTOR IS AT PLAY?

- The CEO's mixed messages
- Competing political agendas on the executive committee
- Competition for scarce resources
- The competition's latest moves or new technology
- Organizational culture or orthodoxies
- Inauthentic communication
- Making hot issues undiscussable

Committed Speaking: Discuss the Undiscussable

The enemy of authentic dialogue is superficial congeniality, where people make the hot or controversial issues undiscussable. This can lead to confusion as to your mandate, miscalculations in your game plan, and blow ups with your boss down the line. It is much better to discuss the undiscussable by asking direct questions: *Boss, how strongly do you feel about building a global brand? ...growing the business? ...developing game-changing products?* If asking direct questions about your mandate raises hackles with your boss, tease out your mandate by asking questions that are less direct.

Committed Listening: From a "Me Point of View" to a "You Point of View"

Committed listening starts with giving people the gift of your presence and listening with a high quality of attention. It also means dropping the tendency we all have to listen from a "me point of view" or your concerns— my job mandate, my department, my budget. It means listening from a "you point of view" where you listen from the perspective of your boss's concerns— his mandate, his goals, his budget. For example, ask questions like: *How do you see your job mandate and what is expected of you? What can I do in my job to help you be successful in yours? Do you have any big requests of me?* Committed listening also involves disconnecting the big filters that prevent one from hearing what the other person is saying — or distorting it. You might hear the boss saying a "yes," when it fact, she is saying a "no" or a "maybe."

PRACTICE AND RELFECTION ASSIGNMENTS

The purpose of the exercises below are first to help you to get clear about people's expectations of you and then to get others clear about your expectations of them.

Practice & Reflection Assignment 1: Get on your boss's schedule to clarify your job mandate or resolve dilemmas. I suggest proactively seeking out a meeting with your boss (and others on the executive team) at the beginning of your first hundred days. It's all too easy to get stuck in a situation where you have to wait for your boss to finish his board meetings, return from his business trip to Japan, and then take his much deserved two week family vacation. I would also suggest getting on the schedule of other key executives, whose support you are going to need to accomplish your goals. If possible, I would ask your boss's secretary to set up a second and third meeting, at the same time, so you don't get locked out due to a packed schedule.

KEY PEOPLE WHOSE SCHEDULE I NEED TO GET ON TO CLARIFY MY MANDATE

- Board members
- CEO
- Members of the Executive Committee
- Head of HR

Practice & Reflection Assignment 2: Write down your mandate. We have used a lot of words to talk about your going-in mandate. I would now like to suggest you take out a piece of paper and write it down in terms of a sentence or short paragraph. Once you write this down, run it by your boss at your next scheduled meeting.

MY MANDATE

- My job title is:
- My basic role, responsibilities, and tasks are:
- My going-in mandate is:
- The impact I am expected to have is:
- I am empowered to accomplish my mandate by doing:

Practice and Reflection Assignment 3: Ask your boss to be a thinking partner in clarifying your mandate and resolving any dilemmas. It would be great if you were the boss, if this was your company and your vision of where to take it, and your rules, but in most cases, it won't be. You have to sort out very early what your going-in mandate is, and one of the best ways to do that is to ask your boss and other movers and shakers in the organization good questions. At the same time, even if you are relatively clear about your going-in mandate, you may be faced with issues and dilemmas. My advice is to ask your boss to be a thinking partner with you in resolving these.

USE YOUR BOSS AS A THINKING PARTNER

- In regard to my going-in mandate, can we clarify a few things so as to insure my effectiveness?
- There are some dilemmas that have arisen about the goals and objectives and I would like to ask you to be a thinking partner with me on this.
- I would also like to talk to you about your leadership style with direct reports and how you would like to work together.
- Can you help me with getting other members of the executive committee on-side?
- There are some unwritten rules and cultural norms I have been wondering about, such as (state what they are), what are your thoughts on these?
- How would you deal with these issues (state specific issues) if you were in my shoes?

Practice and Reflection Assignment 4: Find a coach or mentor who can help you deal with the informal power structure. Your boss and the chain of command represent the formal power structure, but there is also an informal power structure you need to work with. Linda Hudson, President and CEO of BAE Systems as quoted in the New York Times, said that an early boss told her, "Spend the first couple of months in this job figuring out the informal power structure and how things really work around here. Then with the help of a champion or mentor go and establish allies with the real movers and shakers in the organization because that's how you will be successful. Once you catch on to who really pulls the strings and where the real power base is, who you have to collaborate with, who you have to inform, who you have to seek for advice and agreement, you can actually make these big, very, very lumbering organizations work very, very well."[15]

FIND A COACH OR MENTOR TO HELP WITH THE INFORMAL POWER STRUCTURE

- Who are the 5 to 6 people I need on board to fulfill my mandate?
- Set up a meeting with each of the people you will need to support you.
- Describe the mandate you were given and see whether they agree or disagree.
- Ask: What do you see as the breakthrough steps needed to reach it?
- Send up trial balloons. How do you feel about branding, growth, advertising?
- Find out the kinds of things people will support you on and/ or oppose you on.
- Figure out how you can get where you are going by helping others get where they are going.

Practice and Reflection Assignment 5: Learn to work with the unwritten rules of the game. According to Linda Hudson, "I tell people that in a corporate environment, first and foremost you need to understand the unwritten rules of the culture you work in, and find a way to make it work for you rather than trying to fight it."[16] For example, CEO Dave Citrin of Alcatel told his CFO, Bart James, to focus on growth initiatives rather than cost reduction. However, he expected all his managers to follow the unwritten rule to use him as a sounding board, before going off halfcocked.

FIND A MENTOR TO DISCOVER THE UNWRITTEN RULES

- What is the best way to get my boss's or executive committee's approval?
- What are my boss's expectations of someone in my position?
- What are the unwritten rules of the behavior my boss expects me to follow?
- Who does my boss empower and why? Who does my boss disempower and why?
- What receives kudos from other key executive committee members?
- What gets them angry?
- What are the cultural norms for making things happen (for example, building consensus)?
- What are the unwritten rules of the game?

Getting Others Clear About Your Mandate for Them

Now that you are clearer about what's expected of you, let's focus on what others can expect from you. If you are coming in from the outside, chances are that people will have called friends in other companies or Googled you to find out your leadership approach and winning strategy in business, which may be creating some anxiety for people. For example, when Arthur Martinez took over Sears, his reputation was the "Axe from Saks." Martinez turned that expectation around by setting forth a clear vision for Sears around growth and making comments at company town meetings like, "You can't shrink your way to greatness."

Practice and Reflection Assignment 6: Let me introduce myself.
A great way to align other people's expectations is to develop a "let me introduce myself" message. Imagine you are going to be making a presentation at a town hall meeting or executive team gathering that tells people who you are and what to expect from you.

ANSWERS THESE QUESTIONS AS A BASIS FOR YOUR INTRODUCTION MESSAGE

- Who am I?
- Where do I come from?
- Why I am here?
- What do I plan to achieve?
- How will I do this?

Here are some excerpts from Jeff Immelt's introductory speech given at GE's Crotonville leadership center when he first became CEO.

➤ I grew up in a GE household. My father worked for GE for about 40 years in aircraft engines. I've worked for GE for 20 years in plastics, GE Medical Systems, etc.

➤ From this I have developed a couple of passions. I believe in the customer. Every initiative at GE should start from the outside-in vs. the inside-out and be focused on the customer.

➤ Second, I'm a business growth person. I've touched every element of growth from product development to managing sales forces to globalization and business development.

➤ Third, as far as I am concerned, every person at GE is valued, even in tough times. I know that people make the difference in the company and it's very important for a CEO to communicate that.

➤ I have also built some attitudes about what a CEO does. I think of this as the first day of my career, not my last. I will always be measured not by how much I know, but by how much I learn from you.

➤ I believe that the CEO is the chief competitive officer and that the desire to win, the will to win, comes from the top of the company and has to spread throughout the company.

➤ (He then stressed the leadership initiatives he wanted to undertake.) I know where the company is and where it needs to go. But I don't have all the answers...[17]

> *I realized that every first encounter with a Mattel employee had the possibility of being fraught with tension and I wanted to reduce that. Surprisingly, I found that in each situation, recognizing my lack of knowledge about strategy, operations, and culture, while allowing employees to be the boss, actually helped me to lead. - Bob Eckert, CEO, Mattel[18]*

Practice and Reflection Assignment 7: The "Getting to Know You" Process. If you are being hired from the outside, the getting to know you process is a great ice breaker. It's a good way to deal with lingering resentments about why you the job rather than insiders in the company, as well as doubts and anxieties about how you will act in your job, and it will help to establish a spirit of team work early on. Bill Sands, who became a Vice President at Georgia Pacific in charge of operational excellence after it was acquired by Koch Industries, designed this exercise and used it very effectively. Bill thought the dialogue would take thirty minutes. It actually took four hours.

GETTING TO KNOW YOU PROCESS

1. Set up a conference room with three flip charts. At the top of each flip chart, write the following headers:
- *Things I have heard about you.*
- *Things I would like to find out about.*
- *Things I am concerned about.*

For example, I heard you are the kind of leader who likes to talk to people on the front lines. Does that mean you will make decisions without consulting us?

2. Leave the room while the team fills in the blanks anonymously. While you are out of the room, fill out a similar flip chart with your thoughts about the team.

3. When you come back into the room with your flip chart, the dialogue begins.

SUMMARY

- Get clear on your going-in mandate with your boss and others who hired your (board, etc.).
- Address any dilemmas or mixed messages that you find in what people are saying.

- Explore with your boss how you might expand your mandate to include your Impossible Future.
- Introduce yourself to people in the organization: Tell people *who, what, when, why.*
- Neutralize lingering resentments about why you were chosen over others by talking about how smart your colleagues are and showing humility.
- Address doubts and fears. Let people see that you are a real human being who passionately cares about the company and its people.

CHAPTER 3

REALIZE AN IMPOSSIBLE FUTURE AND KEEP YOUR DAY JOB

Make Your Job a Transformational Assignment

THIS CHAPTER IS intended to prepare you for drafting your 100 Day Plan. You should be thinking in terms of an Impossible Future that represents the difference you want to make, as well as how to get the job done on a day-in, day-out basis. In order to set a vision of an *Impossible Future* or succeed in your *Day Job* you will need to establish a baseline that represents were your organization is today and the gaps that need to be filled. You are going to have to understand the current state of your organization (up or down), how well your team is performing against expectations, and the circumstances and conditions of the people your organization touches. *Are voters crying out for jobs? For health care? Better education? Are shareholders, employees, and customers relatively content or ready to rebel?*

KEEP YOUR IMPOSSIBLE FUTURE AND DAY JOB IN A DYNAMIC BALANCE

When Steve Jobs of Apple declared an Impossible Future of changing the world with the personal computer, the mainframe was dominant and most people in the computer industry scoffed at the idea of the PC having any practical application. His Impossible Future was a whole new invented future that would alter all our lives, not a mere goal like increasing profits and growth of mainframes. Think how different all our lives would be without the PC which made the incredibly varied use of the internet possible. Today your PC is your keyboard, telephone, movie theatre, social networking device, and business machine all rolled into one.

At the same time, when Steve Jobs returned to the helm of Apple after a long absence, he had to do what we call his Day Job and get the business on a sound footing. This provided him the foundation for reinventing Apple once more. In 2010, he boldly declared the "era of the PC" over. He declared a new Impossible Future of changing the world with "smart phones" or mobile computing devices. Go to the Apple.com and you will see an ad for the iPhone 4 boldly states *iPhone 4 is here.* It's obvious that the iPhone 4's design has been based on a new paradigm and become a whole new product category that has the potential to be life-altering. It represents a meaningful difference, not just an incremental improvement on the traditional cell phone, and its users attest to this.

Make the Distinction Between *Creating the Business* and *Running the Business*

In both articulating an Impossible Future and planning out your Day Job it is important to make the distinction between *Creating the Business* and *Running the Business*. To realize an Impossible Future, you need to create the business, which means changing the game and taking it to the next level. Yet you also need to focus on running the business, which means getting the fundamentals right.

There is a tremendous opportunity in every country, in every corporation, and in every team or department to create value by being brilliant on the basics—strategy, operations, people management, and customer service. Yet some executives spend their first 100 days and beyond entirely focused on creating the business, coming up with a vision that will drive growth. As a result, they often don't have the necessary wherewithal to invest in their dreams, and come off looking like Don Quixote chasing windmills. Other executives spend all their time on running the business and getting the fundamentals right, but have no vision beyond that and never make any real difference—despite all their effort.

In general, the idea is to transform *Creating the Business* and *Running the Business* into a "both/and" rather than an "either/or" proposition. A business leader who has effectively done this is Jack Welch. When Welch first became CEO of General Electric, it was already a successful company. Yet in New York at the Pierre Hotel on the day he was hire, Welch declared an Impossible Future that represented his main teachable point of view—WINNING.

Welch declared that GE would be #1 or #2 in every business either by fixing, closing, or selling that business. In order to be number one, he told his minions, they had to look for ways to run the business better. This led to programs he initiated like "Work Out," and to GE's famous Six Sigma quality program. At the same time, Welch stressed that to win, every one of the business groups needed to exercise imagination and innovation.

In general, in your first 100 days, you should be focusing on getting the fundamentals of the business right, while polishing up your Impossible Future speech and starting to put the message out there.

INSIGHT INTO YOUR DAY JOB

Your going-in mandate will probably say something about the current state of your organization and what needs to happen to address it. For example, you may have drawn the conclusion that this is a *good* company with strong operations and your mandate is to make it a *great* company by developing innovative products. Or, this business is a growing fast and very profitably and your mandate is to stay the course. Another possibility is that this business is distressed and your mandate is to turn it around with the utmost urgency. In any case, one of the things you will need to figure out starting day one is the general condition of the organization you are taking the helm of, which will tell you a lot about how aggressively you will need to play.

Your going-in mandate will probably focus a lot on doing your Day Job, which usually requires understanding your roles and responsibilities and being brilliant on the basics. For example, if you are hired to run a donut shop, your job will be about making the donuts, making sure customers get waited on, and going to the bank, and so on. The chances are that no one hired you with the expectation to think outside the box, grow the chain through a new franchise scheme, or to come up with innovative game changing products.

At the same time, doing your Day Job and looking for opportunities to *run the business* better can create tremendous value for an organization. One of the first things to in your first 100 days is to not only make sure you understand the goals and expectations required of you, but to do a deep dive investigation of the past and current performance. Are Wall Street, the CEO, employees, and customers reasonably content with the company's performance or is there a crying need to bring about some real change? Engaging in this kind of inquiry will reveal many opportunities for running the business better. Some opportunities for improvement will be urgent, others less so.

One of my clients was hired as a CEO of a Fortune 500 company that was sending out distress signals. The previous CEO was fired over some ethical issues, the stock was dropping like a rock, and the company had lost $100 million in the previous half year. His mandate was to turn the company around, goosing the stock price, getting the company in the black and restoring morale—all of which required running the business better.

He went into the job on a Monday and discovered that the CFO had recently signed off on a very generous benefits plan for the former CEO and executive committee that was nothing short of criminal. The CFO was out by Wednesday. He also cut back an overly generous employee retirement plan that left the company with a billions of dollars in liability on its books. This led to an immediate jump in the stock price.

He also discovered that the company's far-flung manufacturing plants presented many opportunities for operational improvement (lost profit opportunities), but that no one had ever held the plant managers accountable. It seemed that, while there was a high sense of "ownership" in the company due to the employee benefits plan, there was very little accountability. He addressed this during his first 100 days and over the course of the first year, over 100 million dollars began to drop to the bottom line.

A "WHAT'S SO" PROCESS TO UNDERSTAND COMPANY PERFORMANCE

One of the things that my client did to discover opportunities to run the business better was the Masterful Coaching "What's So" process, which is a powerful technique for understanding current and past performance of the business. The *What's So* process involves gathering a diverse team of people from different levels with different views and perspectives for an all-day meeting to do a deep dive on the business. Capture the answers to investigative questions on flip charts.

SOME QUESTIONS TO INVESTIGATE IN THE DEEP DIVE

- *What is our basic mandate as an organization?*
- *What are the facts about this organization, not interpretations?*
- *What has been accomplished recently?*
- *What is working? What is not working (really not working)?*
- *What's missing that, if provided, would make a difference? (new ideas, fresh approaches, innovative solutions)*

By the end of the day, the walls of the room should be covered in flip charts and the opportunities to run the business better are painfully evident. The process should also reveal some fascinating and intriguing opportunities for creating the business, which can later lead to a discussion of the Impossible Future.

THREE BUSINESS PROCESSES TO PAY ATTENTION TO IN THE WHAT'S SO PROCESS

- **The Strategy Process**: *Do we have the right goals and are we on the right road?*
- **The Operations Process**: *What products needed to be produced? What services need to be delivered? How well do our business processes do that?*
- **The Talent Management Process**: *Do we have a good process for talent acquisition, performance, and development? Are people being held accountable for doing the basic blocking and tackling that goes with their jobs?*

Look for Areas with No Business Process or Broken Processes

Going through the *What's So* process will reveal immediate opportunities for making improvements to business processes. For example, I was coaching the head of a marketing and corporate communications group during her first 100 days and beyond. Unfortunately, there was a big PR crisis that happened during the first 100 days and two more over the next year. I noticed that each time there was a PR crisis, everyone ran around like the volunteer of the fire brigade trying to put out the blazing fire that might destroy the whole town.

It occurred to me that there was either no process or a broken process for dealing with a PR crisis. I then coached the executive to design a process that would allow them to: 1) anticipate a PR crisis, 2) deal proactively with the PR crisis when it occurs, and 3) prevent a PR crisis from happening by identifying potential risks in every quarter of the business. This new business process represented a significant change and required the manager to stretch her going-in mandate beyond the traditional area into the sacred control grounds of other departments. I then coached the manager on how to be a change insurgent.

Competitive Benchmark Against Your Industry

> *How do leading companies in your industry run their business or department? Why doesn't your company do it that way?*

One of the important discussions you can have during the *What's So* process or later on involves competitive benchmarking. For example, when President Barack Obama took a stand for a national healthcare system, he asked his team to study the national healthcare system of many different countries. Unexpectedly, China and Cuba ranked very high because the medical systems in these countries was designed to deliver healthcare to the masses, not for doctors and hospitals and health insurance companies to make a profit. This investigation led to the question, "Why don't we do it that way?" Even though taking on what other countries or corporations do may not fit your situation, asking these questions can be very revealing.

Practice and Reflection Assignment 1: Warm Up for Writing Your Day Job Description

Do a first pass where you write down 5 to 10 bullet points to answers each of the questions below.

- *What is your job title and basic job description?*
- *What are the key responsibilities and tasks of anyone with your job (title) in any company in your industry? Is your job the same or different?*
- *What was in your job description when you applied? What was the going-in mandate that you were given when hired for the job?*
- *What are the key deliverables that other people in your organization expect of you?*
- *What breakdowns or improvement opportunities have you noticed?*
- *How do leading nations, corporations, groups deliver that same product or service? Why don't we do it that way?*

Practice and Reflection Assignment 2. My Day Job Description

Now refine your list to come up with a description of your Day Job.
- *My job title and position is:*
- *My going-in mandate (the challenge) that I have the responsibility and authority to act on is:*
- *My basic roles are:*
- *The key deliverables I am responsible for are:*
- *The business processes I am responsible for are:*
- *The breakdowns and opportunities for improvement I have noticed that I intend to impact are:*

Whether your job title is President of Singapore or CEO of Infosys or department head of whatever, you now have a Day Job description that tells you about the basic blocking and tackling you need to do. That Day Job description includes insight into past and current business performance, together with insight about how to run your business better. Though your Impossible Future and Day Job may appear to be in conflict at times, they actually play off each other. You can't go off on a quest to discover a new world if you are in a leaky boat. At the same time, if you only do your Day Job, you will never be more than a mere foot soldier doing his duty in the long march of history. Remember, it is a *both/and* not an *either/or* proposition.

DECLARE AN IMPOSSIBLE FUTURE

> *Create an Impossible Future that takes you from running the business to creating the business.*

We are now going to coach you to be a revolutionary leader by encouraging you to take a stand for Impossible Future that has the potential to alter the course of history. We will support you in writing an Impossible Future Statement during your first 100 days that represents the difference you want to make in your new executive assignment. It will take you from *running the business* to *creating the business*.

Robert F. Kennedy captured the essence of the Impossible Future when he quoted Bernard Shaw, "Some men see things the way they are and say *why?* I dream things that never were and say *why not?*" The Impossible Future represents standing for an exciting new possibility, one that is a radical departure from the status quo. An Impossible Future is often grounded in the miserable circumstances and conditions of one's followers. Think Lech Walesa in the Gdansk shipyards, Nelson Mandela and apartheid, President Barack Obama and the fact that 40 million Americans did not have access to affordable healthcare. Yet just as often, the Impossible Future can be derived from coming up with a fascinating and intriguing idea that has game-changing potential for your business. Think Apple, think Amazon, think YouTube.

The idea for an Impossible Future may be the outcome of paying close attention to things like throbbing human needs and wants, new macro-economic trends on the order of a shift to a global economy, or new breakthroughs in technology. A very powerful question to engage with that can lead to the spark of insight about your Impossible Future is: *What's missing from this picture?* I am not talking about an incremental improvement, but something that is an exciting new possibility. Think along the lines of the Declaration of Independence, FedEx's 24-hour delivery, the iPhone, Viagra, or Facebook.

You may be thinking that it's too early to write an Impossible Future based on the time you have been in the job. If so, just think of this as a first iteration of your Impossible Future, based on what you know right now about the current situation and how it needs to be transformed. As you learn more, you can do further iterations. As I always say, it takes seven iterations to get to brilliance; each iteration takes half as long and doubles the output of the previous iteration.

> *Your Impossible Future represents playing*
> *a big game, and making a difference.*

Acid Test: Is it an Impossible Future or Not?

I am talking here about an Impossible Future that is big and bold, "Change the world with the personal computer," not your typical corporate vision statement like, "Be the biggest and the best." While, an Impossible Future is not a mere goal but a whole new order of things, it is more goal-oriented in nature than the mission statements in most corporations which tend to be more process-oriented. For example, process-oriented mission statements often run along the lines of: "To be the number one provider of xyz goods or services in the world," "To excel at serving our customers' needs," and "To put people first so as to achieve profitable growth on a consistent basis."

What's missing from these statements is an Impossible Future that people can feel like they are ready to conquer the world for, as well as a clear target to shoot for. Oftentimes, flowery mission statements not only sound alike, but really don't tell much about the big bold future you are trying to reach. Neither do they tell people *this is how we intend to win in this business* as "Man on the moon by the end of the decade" so aptly did. What's also missing in many statements are the empowering values that will elevate people to their better selves. The average Joe in a giant corporation is not empowered by such values as being the biggest and the best or consistently achieving profit and growth.

An Impossible Future that speaks to the vision in people's minds and hearts will arouse human aspirations. An Impossible Future that entails empowering values will elevate people to their highest selves and cause them to make sacrifices. A good example is the great moral values the founders of the American Republic cited in the Declaration of Independence of "life, liberty, and the pursuit of happiness." A great leader, like Martin Luther King in his "I have a dream" speech, recognized that values empowered followers, who in turn empower leaders.

EXAMPLES OF AN IMPOSSIBLE FUTURE STATEMENT

- *Man on the moon in ten years.*
- *From third world to first.*
- *#1 or #2 in every business.*
- *Change the world with the personal computer.*

WRITING YOUR IMPOSSIBLE FUTURE STATEMENT

The exercises below are designed for people of different professions and occupations—presidents and elected officials, CEOs and executives in corporations, leaders in healthcare, education, or sports. If the questions don't exactly fit your situation, extrapolate or tweak them until they do. They are designed to help you tease out your Impossible Future based on an understanding of the current situation and how it might be transformed by bringing about intended change.

I suggest that your Impossible Future statement start with a bold declaration that represents the headline. If you already have that, great. If not, go through the exercises either by writing down the answers in in your diary or discussing them with a coach or thinking partner who can help you come to a clearer understanding of your own ideas.

Write a sentence or short paragraph on each of the sections below and flesh them out with some bullet points. Your Impossible Future statement should be written in inspiring and empowering language so as to arouse your team's higher aspirations and motivations. Remember "Technicolor language" gets "Technicolor responses".

Practice and Reflection Assignment 3. White Paper Exercise—What is the current reality your nation, organization, or group faces?

Create a short White Paper that sketches out the results of a *What's So* process on your nation, corporation, department. The value of a White Paper is that it is a written artifact that can be used to create alignment.

WHAT'S SO EXERCISE TO GAIN INSIGHT INTO CURRENT REALITY

- *What are the facts?*
- *What's working?*
- *What's not working?*
- *What are the circumstances or conditions that are intolerable? (to citizens, customers, employees)*
- *What's missing that, if provided, would make a difference?*

Practice and Reflection Assignment 4. Imagine an Impossible Future that you are really passionate about.

Use your imagination and step out into the future. Make some notes about what you have imagined.

- Imagine an Impossible Future where you have made a difference in this job.
- Imagine an Impossible Future where you have successfully stood for a new possibility and transformed the current reality from _____ to _____.
- Imagine an Impossible Future consistent with your organization and human needs and wants.
- What is missing that, if provided, would make a difference in realizing your Impossible Future? (new ideas, fresh approaches, innovative solutions)

Practice and Reflection Assignment 5. Write an Impossible Future Statement.

Write a statement that expresses the kinds of vision and values you stand for and then complete the following sentences.

- *The problem my organization and its people are facing is:*
- *The circumstances and conditions that need to be addressed are:*
- *The Impossible Future I passionately care about is:*
  ("Man on the moon" type goal.)
- *This is a transformation from _____ to _____.*
- *What's missing that, if provided, will make a difference in realizing this Impossible Future is:*

Practice and Reflection Assignment 6. Declare Your Impossible Future

Discover the power of a personal commitment and the power of your word, of just saying it will be. Find a friend, colleague, or partner to make the following declarations to.

- *I declare my Impossible Future of* _____ *possible, despite the difficult facts and circumstances we need to overcome.*
- *I commit to realizing my Impossible Future.*

TO SUCCEED YOU WILL NEED TO BE A TRANSFORMATIONAL AND TRANSACTIONAL LEADER

The ability to realize an Impossible Future and succeed with your Day Job depends on both *transformational* and *transactional* leadership. *Transactional* leadership is often what is needed to get elected, climb the corporate ladder, and succeed with your Day Job. Its focus is not to push the envelope toward a grand vision or strategy, but largely to bring about incremental improvements usually by making deals or trade-offs with others. *Transformational* leadership involves offering a vision of an Impossible Future that speaks to the vision in people's minds and hearts.

I recently watched the movie *Pillars of the Earth* which shows a good example of *transactional leadership.* In the story, a high ranking priest, Waleran Bigod, tells the young, idealistic parish priest Philip: "You are a good man, the smartest young priest in the diocese from what I hear." He asks Philip matter of factly: "Are you ambitious?" Father Philip responds that he wants to do something meaningful with his life. "Do you wish to become a Bishop one day?" Bigod asks, to which the response is "no."

"Would becoming the Prior of this cathedral satisfy you," Bigod inquires, "I can sway the Bishop and the priests in the election if you like. Would you like that?" Phillip answers "yes."

The official then reminds him "politics is a bargain between beggars." He goes on to explain that when the Bishop dies, the monks in his order elect a new one. Phillip gets the point and says, "So if you make me Prior, when the time comes, I will make you Bishop." While the young priest agrees to the bargain, you can see the disdain in his eyes for the older priest and this kind of deal-making, which reveals something important about transactional leadership. The commitment of the leader and follower to each other does not go beyond what is exchanged in the transaction. Still transactional leadership may prove a useful way you to get things done in your first 100 days and beyond.

> *You want to build cathedrals, why can't*
> *you be content with building houses. -Wife*
> *to Tom the Builder, Pillars of the Earth*

Transformational leadership is what is involved in realizing an Impossible Future that raises people to their better selves. It starts with offering a vision that arouses the aspirations and needs of followers and then in turn mobilizes them to action often making great sacrifices. To use the *Pillars of the Earth* story again, the new Prior has to deal with an immediate crisis in his first 100 days, the old cathedral burning to ground and leaving the Priory in chaos. Prior Phillip and Tom the Master Builder demonstrate transformational leadership by getting everyone from the King to the Bishop to the local townspeople involved in the Impossible Future of building a new cathedral which will remind everyone of the glory of God and sanctify human beings the moment they walk in the door.

SUMMARY

- In your first 100 days, you will need to find a dynamic balance between an Impossible Future that represents *creating the business* and your Day Job or *running the business.*
- Do a "What's So" process to better understand the company's performance and gain insight into your current reality.
- Working off of the insight gained in the What's So process, write a Day Job description that clearly defines what you will be doing to run the business.
- Now declare an Impossible Future that will transform current reality and take you and your organization (business or industry) to a whole new place.
- Make sure that the Impossible Future speaks to the vision in people's hearts and minds.
- Write a first iteration of your Impossible Future statement.
- Commit to being a both a *transactional* leader and a *transformational* leader to successfully preform your Day Job and to create your Impossible Future.

CHAPTER 4

DRAFTING YOUR 100-Day Plan

Jump Start Your Impossible Future, Get Bottom Line Results Fast

AS WE SAID in the introduction, this book is for those who want to be a *great* leader, not just a *good* one. In the previous chapters we set the stage for this by encouraging you to declare an Impossible Future that, if achieved, would make a difference. We also encouraged you to not lose sight of delivering on your Day Job and running a tight ship. While it's good to think about lofty things, it's now time to plant your feet on the ground and develop a 100-Day Plan that reflects your goals and priorities on both fronts. The idea is to generate a conversation for action that will result in you having an impact in your first 100 days, one that will allow you to build rapid momentum and impress others that they made the right decision in hiring you for the job.

> *You set the stage for coming up with the 100-Day Plan by understanding your current position, destination, and course of action.*

I love sailing, which teaches how to navigate from point A to point B. The idea of a 100-Day Plan is to start with a destination, know your current position point, and develop a course of action and then like navigating a sailboat, making adjustments to your course as you go along. In the last chapter, I took you through the *What's So* process to help you establish the current position of the organization you are in charge of. If you haven't done a *What's So,* I suggest you go back and do it. In essence, the What's So is designed to tell you: 1). THE PROBLEMS your nation, company, or group is facing that need to be addressed; 2) THE FACTS that help establish that you are not just making this up, but that there is a real need for change; and 3) WHAT'S MISSING that, if provided, will make a difference. For example, what is missing might be: a way to strengthen your country's position in the global economy; an innovative new product category that will create a revenue storm for your business; or tighter cost controls for your organization.

Your 100-Day Plan keeps you focused
on key goals and high leverage actions
versus falling prey to randomness.

The *What's So* process is not only a great way to establish your Point A or current position, but it becomes the basis of establishing Point B, or where you are going if you don't already know it. Once you know what the problem is and what's missing that, if provided, will solve it, you will start to have some idea of your ultimate destination, as well as some of your immediate goals and priorities for reaching it. This becomes the foundation of your 100-Day Plan. This chapter is intended to provide you a template for setting forth your 100-Day Plan, as well as some examples from my experiences in coaching clients that you will be able to relate to or at least extrapolate from.

> *The 100-Day Plan for your Impossible*
> *Future or Day Job doesn't tell you*
> *what to do right up to the last steps,*
> *but it does give you a place to start.*

If you want to realize an Impossible Future or play a big game, you are in fact chasing a goal that cannot be easily planned or scheduled in terms of a typical one-year plan. The idea of a 100-Day Plan is to give you a place to get started, based on what you know right now. This involves thinking backward from your vision, figuring out the missing pieces that need to be put in place, and then coming up with some immediate goals, priorities, and actions you can get started on. I like to think in terms of 100-day catalytic breakthrough projects that will take you to a different place.

> *The intention of the 100-Day Plan is to*
> *get you to jump into action and achieve*
> *some immediate results that will allow*
> *you to discover the path to the result.*

While it's a good idea to think about your longer-range strategic plan, spending too much time on planning can put you into hot water. In a world of change, complexity, and competition, most of the variables a plan is based on will change before you complete the execution. You may wind up spending lots of time planning for a world that at some point will no longer exist, given that there are three billion capitalists, disruptive innovation caused by technology breakthroughs, and rapidly changing customer habits. Finally, planning is done before we start something, which is when we know the least about the path to the result. In reality, we know more what the path to the result is after we take some action and accomplish some things, than before we do so. The idea of a 100-Day Plan is to set some goals and priorities, and then jump into action. This will insure that you not only accomplish something, but that you also learn a lot about the next steps in the process.

> *You will know a lot more about how to reach your goal after taking action and accomplishing something, than before you have even begun.*

DRAFTING YOUR 100-DAY PLAN: THE DIARY OF A NEW CEO

When one of my former coachees, Greg Goff, was hired to be the CEO of a big oil company, one of the first things he did was create a 100-Day Plan. The way he approached this provides a good example of a business executive who designs and uses a 100-Day Plan to have a powerful and immediate impact, rolling over what he had not accomplished to the next 100 days. I will tell his story here to serve as a short cut to creating your own 100-Day Plan, which you can then begin immediately.

Greg's 100-Day Plan

Greg shared with me that he had learned the importance of a due diligence period while we had worked together about eight years earlier, when he was a regional manager in the UK. The combination of his executive talent and Masterful Coaching had led to a big promotion back in the United States and he had a month or so to prepare for the job. I had contacts back in the home office and helped to get him on people's radar screen, and he used this month to get ready for the new job.

When Greg was hired for this new CEO job, he had requested a month to do his due diligence before starting the job. He told me that he started by doing a kind of "brain dump". This is what he told me:

- I wrote down my reflections on what kind of leader I had been in the past and the teachable points of view that had allowed me to take teams and build up a culture of breakthrough and accountability.
- I wrote down everything I knew about the company based on talking to board members during the hiring interviews.
- I wrote down everything I did not know in the form of all the questions I needed to get answered. I engaged people at all levels in these questions.
- I then listed the issues and opportunities I would face as CEO of the company.

The Big Decision: Impact the Bottom-Line Within 100 Days

Looking at the company with fresh eyes during this due diligence period allowed Greg to see some big opportunities which had been hidden in plain view to his predecessor. After spending a good part of a month engaging in questions, Greg saw that it was possible for him to have a powerful and immediate impact on the company. He determined that he was absolutely committed to impacting the financial bottom-line and, if possible, the stock market price of the company in his first 100 days. Once he had made that decision, he was a man on a mission and pulled out all stops, working nights and weekends to accomplish it. Interestingly enough, he knew he was going to have to be both physically and mentally resilient in order to be up to the task in front of him, so in the 30-day period before he started the job, he changed his diet and worked out regularly in the gym. Muscles appeared, the pounds came off, and he got down to his college weight.

Tease Out the 100-Day Plan in 30-Day Increments

Next, Greg wrote down a list of the things he was absolutely going to do in the first 30 days, the things he was absolutely going to do in the first 60 days, and the things he was absolutely going to do in the first 90 days. He told me, "I wrote down the plan, and when the bell went off on day one, I jumped into action."

In essence, Greg spent his first 30 days in the "getting to know you process," together with conducting a complete review of the company's present and past performance, with a view toward making improvements. This included a review of the leadership team, business strategy, operational efficiency, and finances. According to Greg, "There is tremendous value to be created in just running the business better." Greg spent his second 30 days putting his Impossible Future—creating the business—out to the company, as well as putting into play decisions made in the first 30 days and executing like mad. The third 30 days were spent on making sure all this dropped to the bottom-line. After that, he reviewed where he wanted to go, what he had accomplished, what was missing, and created his next 100-Day Plan.

I carried the plan everywhere I went.

Greg told me, "I was constantly reviewing my 100-Day Plan to make sure I was executing well. At the same time, I carried it with me every place I went and shared it with leaders at all levels of the company. This proved to be a very good way of telling people who I was as a leader, what I was up to, and what I expected of them."

The 100-Day Plan included a *Communications Strategy*. "I was determined to communicate my vision, goals, and teachable points of view to everyone in the company. I spent a long time and effort in a series of town hall meetings designed to mobilize people at every level of the organization. There are over 5000 people in the company, and during the first 100 days, I spoke to all 5000 people during these town hall meetings."

> *I started to make unreasonable promises*
> *and requests of direct reports, so as to*
> *address urgent issues and raise the bar.*

Make Unreasonable Promises and Requests

One of the issues that Greg encountered in taking over a company that was somewhat in a state of distress was that the executive benefits were too high, and costs needed to be cut to get the company back in the black on a consistent basis. One of the things he discovered was that executive perks were way too high and they included use of the company plane, membership in country clubs, and company cars.

He called a meeting of his team and provided them with a TPOV. "Look," he said, "we have to spend the company's money like it's our money. My contract says that I can fly on the company jet for business, personal use, and vacations." He then added, "I would never do that." He also told people on his team that if he had a choice to stay in a five-star luxury hotel or a three and a half star hotel, he would always choose to stay in the more economical one.

He then described the excessive executive perks that were creating a culture of entitlement as well as adding to costs and asked, "What do you want to do about that?" He left the room for the team to discuss this. When he came back, the team said that they felt, given the company's condition, the right thing to do was to get rid of these perks. It was the month of June at the time and they said they could get that done by January, which would have given them the summer months at the country club. Greg directed them, "I want it done by July."

A few days later, he pulled his team together again and talked about his vision and his 100-Day Plan for running the business better. He told people, "It is one thing to have a vision that will produce profitable growth in the years ahead, but there is also tremendous value to be created just from running a tight ship." He then announced that each member of the executive team had 30 days to give him a plan for cutting costs by 15% in their department and then another 45 days to implement it. This sent some shock waves through the executives because it meant getting rid of a lot of people. He also asked them to create a plan for making operational improvements to be executed within one year.

Demonstrating Impressive Results

Prior to their quarterly earnings report, Greg notified Wall Street that some big changes were in the wind which would affect the company's bottom-line. Greg had made all the decisions necessary to impact the company's bottom-line and implemented them immediately. The result? The second quarter earnings report showed a big impact to the bottom-line and both the board members and Wall Street analysts were impressed. The stock price shot up in less than 100 days. In so doing, Greg not only showed that he was on the right track for turning the company around, he also set the stage for other big players in the industry to notice, thereby setting up his next career move down the line.[19]

A TEMPLATE FOR DRAFTING YOUR 100-DAY PLAN

As a new leader, your 100-Day Plan is intended to establish your current position or Point A, your destination or Point B, as well as the immediate course of action. It is designed to help you to take high leverage actions that will not only lead to results, but also reveal the next steps on the path to the result. A 100-Day Plan is not a static document, like an old piece of parchment paper, but rather a living, breathing document that will be renewed as you learn more.

In preparation for creating your 100-Day Plan, I suggest you review your Impossible Future Statement and Day Job Statement that we covered in Chapter Three. I also suggest you review the *What's So* process described in that chapter, which will give you a basis for understanding both the problems your organization is facing and some possible solutions.

I have separated the 100-Day Plan template into three parts: I) Due Diligence, II) My Leadership Commitment, III) 100-Day Action Plan.

100-DAY ACTION PLAN

Name:

Title:

Job I have been hired to do:

Key roles, responsibilities, tasks: (Things anyone in this position would have to do.)

Going-in mandate from conversation with boss:

I. DUE DILIGENCE – What's so about your current situation?

1. Things that have been accomplished by this organization recently:
2. The situation:
   - Indicate which kind of situation you are in: start-up, turnaround or crisis, sustaining success, or culture change
   - The "problem" we are facing:
   - The "biggest opportunity":
3. Build the case for change:
4. Strategy to match the situation: (What's missing that, if provided, can make a difference.)
5. My Impossible Future Declaration:
   - I am committed to the possibility of:
   - My Impossible Future is:
   - Results I want to achieve:
   - I will do this by bringing about the following intended change:

II. MY LEADERSHIP COMMITMENT – Who I need to be in order to achieve my goals.

1. Who I am as a leader:
2. What matters to me:
3. Teachable Points of View for succeeding in this business:
4. Attitudes and behaviors I think are important and want to spread:
5. Top goals and priorities for my leadership in my first 100 days are:

III. 100-DAY ACTION PLAN

1. Top three goals or priorities for my Impossible Future for first 100 days:
2. Things I will absolutely do in my first 30 days: (Think in terms of looking for opportunities to run the business better.)
3. Things I will absolutely do in my second 30 days: (Think in terms of creating the business and making immediate improvements.)
4. Things I will do in my third 30 days:

REVIEW 100-DAY PLAN

Your first 100 Day Plan is not set in stone, but more like a living, breathing document. I suggest updating it monthly, based on what you learn as you take action. I also advise integrating your first 100-Day Plan into your schedule and daily planning diary. Focus your time on your top priorities rather than getting swept away by the urgent. Things that you don't actually accomplish in your first 100 days can be rolled into your first year plan. Having said that, focus not on what you are going to do next year or even next month, but on what you are going to do today.

SUMMARY

- Review your Impossible Future Declaration and your Day Job statement.
- Review the findings of the "What's So" process.
- Create a 100-Day Plan using the template offered.
- Communicate the plan to people whose support and involvement you need to accomplish it.
- Make adjustments to the plan as you achieve quick wins and see new openings for action and achievement.

CHAPTER 5

DEAL PROACTIVELY WITH TURNAROUNDS AND CRISIS

Never Waste a Good Crisis

IN YOUR FIRST 100 days, you may discover that you have to put both your Impossible Future and your Day Job aside and throw yourself right smack dab in the middle of dealing with a turnaround situation or a major crisis. Think George Bush and 911, think CEO Alan Mulally and Ford's turnaround, think CEO Brian Moynihan at Bank of America after the Wall Street implosion of 2008. In fact, many newly installed leaders have to deal with some kind of turnaround situation in their first 100 days, even if it is not exactly one of crisis proportions. As Steven Fink points out in his excellent book *Crisis Management*, "Noah built the ark before it started to rain."

> *You may find that you spend most of your first 100 days in over your head dealing with a major crisis.*

Newly installed presidents of nations, CEOs of corporations, hospital directors and other government or organization leaders often find themselves walking into crisis or turnaround situations that absolutely nothing in their background has prepared them to deal with. On the day of his inauguration, President Obama, previously a community organizer and one-term senator, faced a steep learning curve on multiple fronts—the global economic meltdown, the wars in Afghanistan and Iraq, and Iran and Korea going nuclear. He faced a great deal of public pressure to take immediate and effective action, even though there were no easy or obvious answers. He took bold action and was largely successful, never becoming publicly defensive, even though his critics acted as if he could do no right. During that same time period, CEOs Akio Toyoda of Toyota, Tony Hayward of BP, and many Wall Street types all faced major crises but didn't fare as well.

> *The missteps of CEOs whose brands are under attack often make the situation impossible to spin with PR.*

Toyota, hailed for engineering cars so totally reliable that they seem dull, had to bear revelations that its most popular cars suddenly accelerated for mysterious reasons. The energy behemoth BP, which once branded itself as "Beyond Petroleum" an environmental visionary, now faces the grim future with a new identity, "the perpetrator of the most awful oil spill in the history of the United States." And the Wall Street legend, Goldman Sachs, an elite player in the bow tie and white-collar-class, found itself ridiculed in Rolling Stone as "a great vampire squid wrapped around the face of humanity, relentlessly jamming its blood funnel into anything that smells like money." In each case the CEOs lost touch with their own gut level values and capitulated to stress and pressure, making missteps that brought their integrity into question. This, combined with the fact that the companies were under attack over the very traits that were central to their vibrant global brands, made the situation impossible to spin with PR.

> *In emergency turnaround and crisis*
> *situations, leaders often unwittingly take*
> *their organizations to the brink by putting*
> *short-term thinking over long-term thinking.*

Navigating Through a Storm

In his book *Navigating Through a Storm*, Bill George of Harvard University suggests that one of the characteristics of leaders who successfully deal with crisis is their ability to stick to their own "true north," their own inner composite of ideals, beliefs, values that often manifests as doing the right thing — rather than falling prey to personal or organizational defensive routines, by "doing the expedient thing". For example, James McNerney took over Boeing at a time when the company was being fined $650 million for ethical violations that involved absconding with the documents of Lockheed Grumman. Instead of fighting the fine in court, McNerney chose to pay it to demonstrate Boeing was an ethical company. This not only sealed his leadership but had a hugely positive impact on company morale. Contrast this with Akio Toyoda, who in the middle of the "sudden acceleration crisis", offered up Toyota's plan to repair its public image, rather than to insure public safety, which would have been much more appreciated.

> *Don't get trapped in posturing and defensiveness*
> *rather than looking in the mirror.*

Leaders at high levels have big egos, so when criticized for making mistakes that have led to a crisis, they will tend to react with posturing and defensiveness, saying "I am not responsible." The fact is that leaders frequently do bear a high level of responsibility for the mistakes that lead to a crisis, as well as their mismanagement of them. The leader's complicity in things like cars that accelerate and kill drivers, oil spills that destroy the environment and banking policies that reward greed are bad enough, but when compounded with defensive routines like "face-saving moves," "passing the buck," or "covering things up," there are always escalating consequences. To avoid making the crisis worse, the new leader has to be able to look in the mirror and transform defensiveness into learning.

I coach leaders in crisis situations to not be afraid to show their human side and even some vulnerability. Instead of letting a protective shell harden around you in the face of attacks and seeking to appear strong in front of your team, why not reveal your vulnerability? Ask for team member's support. In so doing, you create a climate in which doubts and worries are voiced and unforeseen issues can be tackled sooner, taping the power of multiple minds in a team approach. It may not be easy to do, but showing vulnerabilities appropriately will facilitate you getting the job done.

In Case of Emergencies: What Not to Do

The following are personal and organizational defensive behaviors that must be avoided at all costs.

Seven Steps for Dealing with a Crisis and Turnaround Situation

I put together the following model based on my own experience of watching presidents and CEOs manage crisis over the years, as well as borrowing from the conceptual frameworks of writers like Steven Fink, Bill George, and others.

SEVEN STEPS FOR DEALING WITH A CRISIS OR TURNAROUND

- You are onstage; stay on track with "true north"
- Get people to face reality
- Show up! Act promptly
- Don't do it yourself; tap the power of multiple minds
- Get to fundamental causes and solutions
- Think of the crisis as an opportunity
- Go on offense; don't just play defense

Act like you are onstage all the time,

because you are. -Carly Fiorina

1) You are onstage; stay on track with "true north"

One of the things a new leader constantly needs to do in a crisis is to look in the mirror to see whether they are staying on track with true north (their beliefs, values) or whether they are just coming from survival. We can see from the great stories of presidents, CEOs, and other leaders that, every time a leader starts coming from survival and acts defensively, they wind up in hot water. Think Richard Nixon and erasing the Watergate tapes. Think Bill Clinton, "I did not sleep with that woman." Think the BP chairman, who said, "We want to get this crisis handled so we can get our lives back." To be sure, the leaders mentioned above were people who had principles and values, but they capitulated under stress and pressure to act defensively. A coach or confidant who encourages you to reflect (versus react) can be a vital asset in situations like this.

> *Most organizations are full of*
> *people who are trying to shade or*
> *avoid reality." -Larry Bossidy*

2) Get people to face reality

During the 2008 presidential campaign, when the whole American banking system was on the verge of collapse and the country was heading towards the biggest recession since the Great Recession, John McCain made the statement that the American economy was "fundamentally sound". Likewise, I wonder what the CEOs of great companies like AIG, Bank of America, Morgan Stanley, and others were thinking and doing a year before the crisis hit? Couldn't they see that their short-term thinking behind things like subprime mortgages was going to result in a boomerang effect? By contrast, great leaders encourage realism. Says Larry Bossidy, "When I took over as CEO of AlliedSignal, I got two different views of reality from our people and our customers. While our people were saying that we were delivering an order-fill rate of 98%, our customers thought we were at 60%. The irony was, instead of trying to address the customers' complaints, we seemed to think we had to show them that we were right and they were wrong."[20]

> *80% of life is just showing up. -Woody Allen*

3) Show up! Act promptly

On Monday, when the hurricane smashed through New Orleans, President Bush took Air Force One to Arizona and California to discuss Medicare. On Tuesday, the day the levee broke, Bush took off to San Diego to speak to World War II veterans. On Wednesday, he flew over New Orleans on the way to a speech at the Rose Garden. On Thursday he made comments on ABC's "Good Morning America". On Friday, as the federal response reached the Gulf Coast, so did Bush. He got an overview of the scene from a cushy seat in a helicopter. The moral of the story? A new leader's track record can be forever marred as a result of not showing up and acting promptly in responding to a crisis. To avoid this, a new leader has to be willing to sit up and take notice when the fire alarm rings, rather than assuming it's a false alarm or not that important. Both in crisis and turnaround situations, my best advice for the new leader is to show up on the scene and take strong action within 24 hours.

Two heads are better than one:
create your own "brain trust."

4) Don't do it yourself; tap the power of multiple minds

When FDR came into office, the country was plunging deep into the Great Depression. Between the time of his election and his inauguration, he put together his "Brain Trust" and would spend most of his day talking to a wide range of people. At the end of the day, FDR would have his bath drawn and then summon his eldest son, James R. Roosevelt, who was his unofficial sounding board. It was during his conversations with his son that he got the idea that one of his most crucial tasks was to say something that would restore public confidence. This led to the Fireside Chat where he reassured people, "The only thing we have to fear is fear itself." He also realized that, while there was no packaged solution or ultimate answer to the problem of breadlines and unemployment, he had to do something. This led to declaring a national bank holiday which gave him time to stabilize the banking system with the FDIC and a torrent of various make-work programs.

5) Get to fundamental causes and solutions

A number of years ago, I was coaching the country manager for Adidas in the USA market. The company was losing money by the bucketful. One day I was in a meeting with the country manager about a turnaround plan, when he got a phone call from the Adidas CEO, Rene Jaeggi, who said that the German mother company was not going to bail the USA company out, "We are not going to send even one pfennig!" The country manager, an able turnaround manager, did his best to stem the tide by tightening advertising budgets and cutting non-performing costs. However, the company continued to lose ground because fundamental causes and solutions had not been addressed—the brand advertising "We are the originals" was pale next to Nike's "Just do it." Furthermore, while people liked the traditional styles of shoes and textiles of the three stripe brand, they looked tired next to Nike's Air Jordans. Finally, deliveries were too slow—most of which were mother company issues, not local ones. It's important to not only deal with fundamental causes and solutions, but to also prepare for the long haul.

6. Think of the crisis as an opportunity

Machiavelli once said to never waste a good crisis. The obvious thing for leaders to do when crisis emerges is to go on the defensive with PR and emergency measures. The non-obvious thing is to see the crisis as an opportunity to begin transforming the organization into one with the right goals and the right governing values. During Chrysler's 1980s crisis, CEO Lee Iacocca took charge, restoring consumer trust in Chrysler which led to a decade of prosperity. When General Motors emerged from bankruptcy in 2010, Chairman Ed Whitaker became the trustworthy, determined face of the company's comeback.

7) Go on the offensive and win; don't just play defense

Alan Mulally came from Boeing to become CEO of Ford in 2006 just before the global financial crisis was about to occur. Because he realized that the company was in a crisis situation due to a down market, he went out and borrowed $26 billion in cash. When GM and Chrysler asked for bailouts two years later, Mulally said that Ford was in a strong condition and could weather the storm on its own. During those two years (2006 to 2008) Mulally sold off non-performing divisions, he retooled plants, and he refocused the company on building cars for global consumers. When Toyota's reputation hit the skids with the accelerator problem, Mulally was ready to go on the offensive with the next generation of Ford cars, including the Focus which provided superior driving quality and exceptional fuel economy. Today, the projected ten-year value of a Focus is significantly higher than that of the Toyota Corolla.

Every New Leader Eventually Faces a Turnaround Situation

When a new leader comes into the job, they usually go through the kind of due diligence process described in the previous chapter, one that involves talking to Wall Street types, board members, customers, employees, and constituents about the issues and opportunities facing the organization. This should lead first to insights about what the problem is and what needs to change, and then to setting goals and priorities. In some cases, a leader's sense of urgency in dealing with the situation will come from the outside in: angry voters, falling stock prices, product recalls, rapid employee turnover, or customers jumping ship.

> *Sometimes the urgency to drive a turn-*
> *around comes from the outside in; at*
> *other times from the inside out.*

In other cases, the so-called turnaround situation will be more determined by the leader learning about a problem that may not be a crisis now, but that may develop into one if not addressed. It could even be a situation where nary a higher up or customer is complaining, even though the group is performing sub-optimally. In this case, the urgency to turn the situation around has to come from within, rather than from external circumstances.

For example, when I coached Under Secretary of Defense John Young, who was in charge of the Pentagon's $350 billion acquisition program, he discovered a smoldering turnaround situation when he learned that the Army, Navy, and Marines were often developing the same weapons, adding billions in unnecessary cost and complexity. Further, similar guns did not have interchangeable parts and communications systems (such as two-way radios) had different technologies that prevented soldiers, sailors, and marines from thinking as a team or interacting in battlefield conditions.

Young decided to do everything within his power to turn this situation around, even though generals in the Army, Navy, and Marine Corps were relatively okay with it. It was not more than a few weeks into his first 100 days in the job, that he created a source document and implementation plan that emphasized the vision of "being able to defeat any enemy, on any battlefield, anywhere in the world," something that would require joint weapons development programs and would eliminate complexity and burgeoning costs.

He also started holding joint meetings with the three services on every key weapons system to ensure that the requirements were aligned and the whole acquisition process went smoothly. This not only had an impact on programs like the Joint Strike Fighter, but many smaller ones as well. One time, Secretary Young came into the meeting and placed three different sets of incompatible walkie-talkies on the table to emphasize his point that the three different services didn't talk to each other.[21]

TIPS FOR DEALING WITH CRISIS AND TURNAROUND SITUATIONS

1. Take a pounding, then get back to work.

In most cases, the standard approach of CEOs and their like in dealing with a crisis is to protect themselves or try to get out in front of the story with PR. However, in most cases the plain truth speaks for itself and the company often looks all the worse for the PR effort. I suggest that if your company is in crisis situation, you should acknowledge even the most awful facts, take responsibility for making things right, take a pounding and then get back to work. The fact is that the CEOs and companies who handle crisis well are the ones you hear little about because they do just what I suggested above. The story may appear in the news, then disappears after a few days, not with a bang but with a whimper. The classic case is when the CEO of Tylenol admitted the OTC drug was poisoning people and then pulled millions of bottles off the shelf immediately.

Ask yourself: *What is the crisis you are facing? (Just stick to the facts.) Are there any ways in which your leadership acts have led to the crisis or made it worse? What awful truths do you need to acknowledge to the world? What would doing the right thing be?*

2. Create Your Own Mastermind Group

President Kennedy made three vitally important decisions during the very first hour after examining the photographic evidence that showed Russian missiles in Cuba: 1) He pulled together a "Mastermind Group" of 15 people who were tasked with coming up with a breakthrough solution to the crisis; 2) He said everyone in the group would be required to radically restrict any information they had from the public about the crisis until the President was prepared to respond to it; and 3) The Mastermind Group was directed to assemble immediately without the President present, to come up with a recommendation for action. They were not to bring a recommendation to the President until all of them agreed unanimously on the course of action to be taken. The group spent 13 days and many hours deliberating on what to do, with the fate of the world hanging in the balance. This story illustrates that while most leaders are highly reactive, when the stakes are high, it's sometimes better to take a reflective stance.

Ask Yourself: *Who are the people you would like in your own mastermind group? What positions do they represent in the organization? Does it include enough outside expertise? Devise some ground rules for how you want this group to think and interact together.*

3. It's Not a Perfect Plan: *Don't just stand there; do something*

When President Barack Obama was elected President, he inherited more crisis situations than any president since FDR (again a banking crisis plus two wars). Poor leadership in government that extended credit irresponsibly — combined with the greed of some corporate CEOs — had sparked a global financial meltdown. Once-venerable banks like JP Morgan, Chase, and Lehman Brothers were teetering on the verge of collapse. General Electric and other corporations that had once been considered the backbone of the American economy were heading toward bankruptcy, and millions of Americans were being thrown out of work. President Obama's first hundred days were spent putting together a team of experts who could reverse this crisis, and coming up with a concrete plan, while the world held its breath. As you know, this led to the banking bailout. There was a public outcry that the government should not put public money into saving institutions that had duped them. President Obama said something that I think anyone dealing with a crisis ought to keep in mind: "There is no perfect plan."

Ask yourself: *Who do you know who could be a coach or confidant, or arm-around-the-shoulder to help you weather the storm? Who could be part of your mastermind group to work together to put together a plan of action? (Again, include people with different views and perspectives who have value to add.)*

4. Jump into Action—Don't Procrastinate

Winston Churchill once said, "The era of procrastination, of half-measures, of soothing and baffling expedients, of delays is coming to its close. We are entering an era of dramatic change." Sir Winston also said that such an approach would have the most dire consequences. This is probably good advice for you. Once you figure out the crisis you are facing, start to come up with an action plan. FDR was coming up with an action plan to deal with the banking crisis within 72 hours of taking office. You may have more than 72 hours, but coming up with a credible action plan in a short amount of time will be a worthy exercise.

Ask yourself: *What does your gut tell you about the crisis you are facing? Are you ready to initiate drastic change? Are you tempted by a half measure? What can you start with right now?*

SUMMARY

- Most leaders have to deal with a crisis or turnaround situation in their first 100 days.
- Show up on the scene and let people know you are taking the crisis seriously within 24 hours.
- Don't get defensive, take responsibility.
- Stick to your ideals, beliefs, and values rather than doing the expedient thing.
- Bring together a "mastermind group" to help you to address the crisis.
- Get to fundamental causes and solutions.
- Come up with an action plan that you can begin to implement immediately.

CHAPTER 6

BUILD A TEAM OF 'A' PLAYERS

Get Me The Best In The World!

WHAT MAKES THE New York Yankees (a baseball team with 40 Pennants and 27 World Series Championships) the New York Yankees? What makes General Electric (a large company that is a consistent winner in almost every far-flung business unit) General Electric? What makes Apple Computer (a company that consistently comes up with *wow* products) Apple? What makes Google, Google? I assert that in each case, it's the commitment of top executives to be on a nonstop quest to recruit, coach, develop, and keep 'A' players in every key job, no matter what the cost.

When Arthur Blank co-founded Home Depot—a company that was destined to transform the home improvement business—back in 1997 and he had a job opening for, let's say, the CFO or marketing vice president or operation's manager, he would personally call up a search firm and say without the slightest hesitation, "Get me the best in the world." Then he would call the best people they suggested, often offering them lots of opportunity and a whopping salary and stock options. Contrast this to all the bureaucratic hoops the typical executive has to jump through in order to hire even mediocre people for his or her team.

As Jack Welch once said, the team with the best talent usually wins. This is true in sports, in the performing arts, and it is certainly true in business. Of this you can be certain: your ability as an executive to turn in a winning performance in your new role will depend less on coming up with the right strategy or organization structure than whether you are able to get the right people on the team bus.

One of the things you can do to assure a winning performance is to make a bone-deep commitment to yourself to build a team with an 'A' player in every key job, even if you don't reach the goal. While it's okay to have some 'B's on your roster, you certainly aren't going to be successful with a team of chronic 'C's. Diagram 6.1 defines an 'A', 'B', or 'C' player.

Diagram 6.1 What is an 'A', 'B', or 'C' Player?

A	Rock star of talent; performs above and beyond the ordinary; game changer and difference maker
B	Delivers consistently acceptable performance; usually the work horse of the organization
C	Delivers erratic performance; full of reasons and excuses; are a psychic drain on bosses

WILL THIS TEAM MAKE IT?

Your first 100 days is at the very least an opportunity to begin grading the people on your team and, if possible, up-grading them as well. This is in part a process of direct observation of people at work, learning to trust your intuition, and seeking opinions from those who know the people on your team better than you do. Let me point out however that building a team of 'A' players in a big organization is not as straightforward as it may sound and is fraught with psychological, political, and financial issues. Ask yourself: *Do I have the courage to make tough people decisions? Am I willing to go head-to-head with HR and other cultural forces that tend to protect mediocre players? Can I come up with the budget to get the rock stars of talent I will certainly need?*

SPORTS PROVIDES A GREAT METHAPOR

I think sports provide a great metaphor for what we are talking about here. In sports, the General Manager of a team—like the Boston Red Sox or New York Yankees—is expected to find the rock stars of talent necessary to win the championship and is constantly faced with grueling public scrutiny in the performance of the job. This job requires the Wisdom of Solomon in making trades and a passion for developing high-potential talent, combined with the capacity to make tough people decisions. The general manager and the coach must trade for 'A' players, have a passion for transforming high potential 'B' players into 'A's, and they must be able to release 'C' players without the least bit of sentiment.

In business, a CEO or executive who thinks and operates like a GM in sports would be immediately accused of engaging in Corporate Darwinism. This is because many corporations lack CEOs and executives who are committed to actually building a winning team, one that has the capacity to be the World Series champions of their industry. In many companies, there is a culture of paternalism that prevents seeking an 'A' player and accepts 'B's and 'C's as if this were their fate. If you are thrown into a new executive role that includes taking an organization to the top or turning around a poor performing organization, this kind of paternalistic thinking will be the kiss of death.

Let me share with you a story from my experience that shows the challenges of dealing with this issue. I was asked by the Chairman of Adidas to coach the executive team of Adidas USA at a time when the company was bleeding cash. I grew to admire and respect all the people on the team as they worked to create a success in Adidas USA. Then unexpectedly, the Chairman, an emotional leader who had a hard time making tough people decisions, especially with people he liked, turned the reins of Adidas USA over to Peter Ueberroth, a star-studded entrepreneur who had managed the USA Olympics in Los Angeles, turning a profit for the Olympics for the first time.

Ueberroth came in on his white chariot and met with the team I was coaching. After the meeting, he called the Chairman and said, "This team isn't going to make it." He had the guts to fire the whole team after one meeting. The larger issue was that Ueberroth installed a COO named Peter Perner, who turned out to be worse than the one who was fired, and the company continued to lose money. Ueberroth didn't devote the time and energy necessary to build a team of 'A' players. His assessment of the existing team was based on jumping to conclusions, and he actually fired one or two rock stars of talent. Within a year, Ueberroth and Perner were both gone.

ASSESSING YOUR TEAM

Step 1. Review the Organization Structure

Typically, new executives come into an organization and start fiddling with the organization chart. The modus operandi behind this often has more to do with solidifying the executive's powerbase than it does with building a winning team. There is usually a call to arms around the corporate flag, "One brand, one company," with corporate dominating the divisions in the hinterlands. In other cases, Business Unit leaders in far flung regions fight for their independence, "We know our market and our customers."

There also are usually fights around whether to create a vertical functional organization or a horizontal cross-functional one.

In Your First 100 Days, Review the Organization Chart

1. What is the company strategy? Will the organization structure help realize this?

2. What are the key positions on the organization chart relevant to your job?

3. Do you have the right people reporting to you? Are there too many or too few?

4. Does the current organization structure facilitate teamwork or warring tribes?

5. What alternatives do you see to the current organization structure?

Step 2. Evaluate the Players in the Key Positions on Your Team

Look at the key positions on the organization chart and identify the ones where you absolutely need an 'A' player (or at least a very high 'B') to succeed in your job. Then, from your first days in the office, begin evaluating how the players in your organization stack up. Learn to trust your intuition, but validate it with other opinions and performance data if possible. Make some notes, and if possible, find someone to think out loud with. Diagram 6.2 is a sample evaluation of a team.

Diagram 6.2 Evaluate Your Team Players

Sam CFO	B	Good bean counter and controller, but does he have what it takes to pull off the deals we need to make?
Joe Marketing	A	At only 36, seems like a rock star of talent; get him a coach
Harry Supply Chain	C	Nice guy, keeps things humming, but if it is vital to shake up suppliers in order to reduce costs, he may have to go; think about changing his role
Lisa Project Manager	A (potential)	Smart, young, asks provocative questions and delivers results; coach her to make the shift from manager to executive
Tom Sales Manager	Chronic C	Makes a good impression, but hasn't delivered for the last 6 quarters, even with our most competitive products and despite having a coach; fire him

Step 3. Decide Who to Coach, Redeploy, or Release

You are not going to make these calls in week one, but as you can see from the above, you can come up with at least a preliminary game plan.

THINGS TO KEEP IN MIND WHEN EVALUATING TEAM

1. Beware of people on your team who are good at managing impressions, but who don't add a lot of value. I was working for a

big defense contractor in Washington DC, where the CEO had recently resigned and an interim CEO had been installed. The interim CEO was a highly respected four star general, previously in charge of Central Command (Centcom) during the Clinton administration. The interim CEO went through his standard operating procedure of evaluating the people on his team. He confided to one trusted advisor, "There are too many long-faced engineers in gray flannel suits in charge of Business Units around here who don't think strategically." That was pretty much obvious to all, as the company was less fitted for innovation than it was for improving on what already existed.

Yet evaluating the people on the corporate staff proved more difficult. There was one Senior Vice President of Government Relations (a key role in the Defense Industry) who I will call Mike, who was a charming, smooth-talking Washington insider, great at polishing his own star, but if truth be told, he came up short on delivering added value. The interim CEO, in his previous role as a board member for the company, had known Mike and had become susceptible to his charms, one of which was to name drop in order to point out what a good job he was doing at his role in PR.

"I was just talking to General Petraeus about that..." or "I was talking to Secretary of Defense Gates about this..." Or "They all hold you (Mr. CEO) in the highest regard and think we are a great company." This was just what the CEO, who had an outsized ego, wanted to hear, so the fact that Mike was merely managing impressions did not really occur to him.

One day it came to the interim CEO's attention that Mike was involved in a power struggle with Barb, the Senior Vice President of Corporate Communications, Media, and Advertising. It was obvious that Barb was an 'A' player and in many ways a rock star of talent. She had been very innovative in coming up with an advertising campaign that portrayed the defense contractor as not just making things that go boom, but as also doing some things that made a better world—providing electricity, clean water, jobs in Africa and other places—consistent with the incoming Obama administration's foreign policy. Barb's justification for this ad campaign was that people inside and outside the beltway didn't really know what the company stood for, which clearly threatened Mike.

You guessed it, the interim CEO, former four star general, head of Centcom sided with his old buddy Mike. He was overwhelmed by Mike's ability to manage impressions. In a short time, Barb was given her walking papers.

2. Beware of HR managers who are 'C' players and who protect other 'C's. Let me tell you that in my experience, going through a team evaluation exercise like this can be an eye opener. It requires that you (and other people in the organization who may help you with it) have a commitment to the truth, rather than a commitment to protecting people. Let me share with you another story from my experience in coaching executives.

I was asked by the new CEO of Cadbury Schweppes USA, who I will call Joe, to fly out to Dallas to talk to him in his new role. When I asked him what his goal was, he replied, "To grow the business by leaps and bounds." The business had grown over the previous years, but mainly through acquisition. His leadership and business challenge was to grow the business organically.

I asked Joe to show me his organization chart and to designate the most key leadership roles, as well as to indicate how many 'A' players he had to fill those roles. Joe went through this process out loud and then said he had no choice but to conclude that out of 10 people on the executive team, he had maybe one 'A,' one 'B,' and the rest were chronic 'C's. It was an eye opener for him.

Joe took pause for a moment and said, "This is really surprising. Let me get a second opinion." He called in Frank the HR Manager and asked, "How many 'A' players do we have on this executive team?" Frank thought about it for a minute or so, then said unequivocally, "We have ten out of ten 'A' players." He then added, "I ought to know, I hired them."

Joe confided in me later that this statement by Frank led him to the conclusion that Frank didn't have very high standards and was perhaps a 'C' player himself. This story illustrates how important it is to hire HR Managers who are themselves 'A' players.

3. Find talent scouts whose people judgments you can trust, and ask some pointed questions. During the course of meeting and greeting people in your new job, you will most likely run across certain people who are good talent scouts and who will give you an opinion about the people on your team you can take to the bank. I am talking about talent evaluators who themselves have a commitment to the truth and who will tell it like it is. However, it is still very important to ask these people questions that will help you to sort out who are the 'A's, 'B's, and 'C's.

I was coaching a division president, George, at an oil company who had just been given a promotion. George's first task after coming up to speed on the numbers of the business was to find out how many 'A' players he had on his leadership team, as well as in the next level down. George accomplished this by asking a few simple but pointed questions of his own people. For example, "Bill, you have Charlie on your team in exploration and production. Do you consider Charlie to be an 'A' player?"

Bill's response to the question was "Yes, of course Charlie is an 'A' player. He made his numbers this year." George said, "great" and came back with a second question. "Can you tell me anything Charlie has done in the last several years to make a difference? Can you tell me anything Charlie has done to be a real game-changer as reflected in results?"

At that point Bill, who considered Charlie a friend, said something like "Of course Charlie has made a difference. Of course he has changed the game." Yet when George came back with, "Tell me exactly what Charlie has done to make a difference and be a game changer," Bill had nothing to say. This story again illustrates that one way of figuring out how many 'A' players you have on your executive team is to ask those players to evaluate the people on their own team.

THINGS TO DO AND PITFALLS TO AVOID

As we can see from the above example, building a team of 'A' players can prove not only challenging, but tricky. Here are some tips that can help you in the process:

- **Let people on your team know that you intend to be a team player and that you expect team play.** Your first 100 days is a great time to send a message that you intend to be a team player yourself and to let people know that you expect them to be team players as well. Team effort will be praised. Non-team behavior, like sabotage and undermining, will not be tolerated.

- **Develop your own list of criteria for what constitutes an 'A,' 'B,' or 'C' Player.** Performance matters, but you may also want to take into account how well the person shows up as a leader. Also consider how well they live the governing values of the organization, like passion, commitment, zeal, honesty, integrity and so on. You can also use this assessment as a basis for coaching people.

- **Hold a yearly talent review with your team.** Spend at least one full day a year with your team to evaluate who are the 'A,' 'B,' and 'C' players in your organization. Make sure you encourage everyone present to give their candid opinions. Gathering different views and perspectives on an individual, as well as debating people's different perspectives is a good way to make sure your evaluation of people is objective.

- **Determine to spend 20 to 30 percent of your time coaching and teaching.** You will never be able to simply hire all 'A' players for your team. First, they are expensive and second, stealing them away from the competition won't be easy. You have to take the time to coach people with the highest potential to break through to the next level—from manager to executive, from being a 'B' player to being an 'A' player.

- **Send out Talent Scouts.** Many leading organizations reward employees with substantial bonuses for seeking out top talent and introducing them to the organization. How about doing the same?

SUMMARY

- To create an Impossible Future and excel in your industry you need to have a nonstop quest to recruit, coach, and keep an 'A' player in every key job.
- Ask yourself: *Will this team make it?*
- Review the organization chart and assess the key roles and the people in them.
- Evaluate your team players: Are people an 'A', 'B', or 'C'?
- Decide who you need to coach, redeploy, or release.

CHAPTER 7

MASTER THE POLITICAL CHESSBOARD

Look Both Ways, Don't Get Hit By a Bus

PRESIDENT JOHN F. Kennedy once pointed out how important it was to gain high office if you wanted to realize an Impossible Future and make a difference. He observed that the President of the United States could accomplish more in one day with the sweep of a pen than he could in a decade in the Senate. Yet, gaining power and influence is not enough to make you a master politician. Just consider the number of presidents of countries, CEOs of corporations, general officers in the military, chancellors of universities, coaches of sports teams who got to the top, but failed to leave a lasting legacy of irreversible change.

> *Every mother wants her son to be president,*
> *but no mother wants him to become a*
> *politician in the process. -John F. Kennedy*

GETTING TO THE TOP IS NOT ENOUGH

Having the ability to realize an Impossible Future and also succeed in your Day Job requires using your first 100 days to begin mastering the political chessboard. I am not just talking about newly installed presidents of countries or CEOs of big businesses, but also the new leaders in any organization of more than five people. The fact is, the closer you get to the top, the more competition there will be for power and scant resources. Your triumph or defeat against opponents to get to the next rung up the ladder or to get your plan or budget approved depends more on how effective you are in swaying powerbrokers to back you and campaigning for people's hearts and minds, than it does on how much rational sense your plan makes on paper to you and your inner circle. In my work with executives, I have observed so many times that, when organizations don't do the rational thing, it is all about politics, not reason.

What does it take to be a master politician? It involves knowing who you are and what you stand for and convincing others to "vote for change," as well as knowing the path to power in your situation. It not only means currying favor with bosses and befriending colleagues who will watch your back, but also winning over people at all levels. It involves knowing what moves to make in order to master the political chessboard in the midst of conflicting agendas, shifting power networks, and unexpected turns of events. As James MacGregor Burns said about FDR in accomplishing his New Deal, his success in politics came from being able to "move like a creative artist amongst the tangle of conflicting forces and confusing interests." The worst mistake you can make is to assume that you don't have to be a politician or that politics doesn't exist.

Realizing an Impossible Future and Delivering on Your Day Job: *It's All Politics!*

George Washington, Thomas Jefferson, Benjamin Franklin, Abraham Lincoln, Franklin Delano Roosevelt, Mahatma Gandhi, Winston Churchill,

Martin Luther King, Nelson Mandela, Lyndon Baines Johnson, and Ronald Reagan were all master politicians. People who govern in war and peace do politics. Leaders who change the game in business do politics. Scientists who win the Nobel Prize for their research do politics. Activists who lead the charge to improve community schools do politics. Even great artists who represent a new school do politics. So why not you?

My work involves coaching executives both in business and government: presidents, CEOs, and vice presidents, service secretaries and so on. We spend the first one third of our year-long coaching program helping people formulate the Impossible Future and winning game plan, while making sure that the things they need to do to deliver on their Day Job don't fall through the cracks. We spend the second third of the year helping people develop the political savvy they need to master the political chessboard they are on (a full third of the year) so they can move their agenda forward. The last third of the coaching process is on execution.

> *Moving your agenda forward on the*
> *political chessboard involves moving like*
> *a creative artist amongst the tangle of*
> *conflicting forces and confusing interests.*

Gain Insight into Your Political Chessboard

Coaching someone to realize an Impossible Future and master the political chessboard involves guiding them through the maze of time and space. One of the things I suggest to coaches in their first 100 days is to use the opportunity to meet and greet people in order to gather information about the key players, shifting power networks, and conflicting interests on the company's political chessboard as it exists today. It is important to reverse your usual statement-to-question ratio when in conversation in order to learn. It's amazing what people will tell you just because you asked them a question.

Questions to Ask to Gain Insight Into the Political Chessboard

- *What is the chief executive's or boss's agenda?*
- *What are the biggest opportunities and challenges we face?*
- *Who has real power on the executive team and who doesn't? How is this changing?*
- *How do the positions and interests of the people on the executive team vary?*
- *Where are the conflicts?*
- *Who are the fair-minded colleagues I can trust? Who are the sharks circling for blood?*
- *What expectations do people have of me and my group?*
- *What can I do to help people be successful?*
- *How can I get noticed in a favorable light?*
- *What attitudes or behaviors will unwittingly get me into trouble?*
- *Who can mentor me?*

It is important to reverse your usual statement-to-question ratio when in conversation in order to learn.

As a newly installed executive, you need to start building a shared vision and mobilize people to take action early on in the game. At the same time, you must not forget that every move you make is going to take place on the political chessboard, where the questions just asked will help provide you more understanding. Thus, the clearer you are about the players on the political chessboard and how their ideas and agendas might impact yours, the less likely you are going to wind up bumping into obstacles you didn't know were there.

> *Each step you take to realize your*
> *goal is likely to create a widening*
> *arc of support and opposition.*

A typical scenario for you as a new leader might be that you spend time building a shared vision and action plan, coming up with a beautiful PowerPoint presentation for the executive committee. You may receive kudos from the CEO, verbal support from others, and even tacit nods from those you thought would oppose you. It's a step in the right direction, which some describe as an "evolutionary change." Yet as time goes on, the things you do as a result of this encouragement may cause others to think that what you are up to is not evolutionary change, but revolutionary change.

People may feel that the leadership authority you are demonstrating based on your vision or 100 Day Plan threatens to shatter their leadership authority and area of control. Or they may feel that the success of your proposal will encroach on their resources or sacred control ground. If so, you may soon discover that each step you take to realize your goals and bring about change creates a widening arc of both support and opposition. The dynamics of mastering the political chessboard, at this point, present you with the need to make your moves with skill, creativity, and wisdom.

Map the Political Chessboard

You will be in a much better position in your first 100 days and beyond if you have taken the time to map out the political chessboard, a necessary precursor to deciding your next moves. An exercise I usually suggest to my coaching clients is to take out the organization chart and mark it up with the following four categories in mind.

Look at Your Organization Chart and Ask

- Who are my likely supporters?
- Who are my opposers?
- Who are the neutrals (on the fence)?
- Who are the passives (people who have a view, but don't act on it)?

Once you do that, you need to look at what you can do to build support, overcome opposition, get people who are neutral onto your side, or get friendly passives to take action.

In most cases, the next move in mastering the political chessboard, once you map it is to set up a meeting where you can sit down around the table with some of the key players. You may be able to get potential supporters on your side by arousing people's aspirations and needs. For example, Steve Jobs recruited former Pepsi executive John Sculley as CEO of Apple by asking, "Do you want to change the world or spend the rest of your life making colored sugar water?" You may be able to deal with opposers by putting aside ideological rifts and wheeling and dealing, or cutting deals that are mutually beneficial.

When Shimon Peres was the Foreign Minister of Israel, he told me that during the first negotiations with the Palestinians prior to the Oslo Peace Accords, he would go to secret meetings with Palestinian leaders at three in the morning. One of the first things he learned was that "the enemy doesn't have horns on his head." The next thing he learned was that, "even if the two sides had big differences, there was common ground, like security." Nobody wanted their children to be blown up by a bomb while they were playing in the schoolyard or street. This led to some very positive proposals which became the basis for the successful negotiations at Oslo. Unfortunately, these were dashed due to the assassination of Yitzhak Rabin and the installment of a new hawk government.

Negotiating Tactics on the Political Chessboard

- Sound the high note: a higher goal that unites all. *We all want to build a great nation, business, etc.*
- Honor the different players and their different perspectives
- Start the meeting around a specific problem
- Seek first to understand
- Focus on interests rather than positions
- Build common ground; create an action plan
- Don't burn any bridges

Most presidential candidates are tough guys.
They have to be, especially when they lose.

DEALING WITH A DIVIDED SYSTEM OR STRUCTURAL CONSTRAINTS

The founding fathers of the United States endowed the nation with the Declaration of Independence and the US Constitution. However, they also endowed the nation with a divided system of government that was intended to provide checks and balances on power. Citizens may elect wonderful leaders to be President of the United States, but it has proven very challenging for any president to govern effectively once in office, given just how difficult it is to knit the different pieces of government together and actually get something done.

Just think about how many successful presidents there have been in history, or in your own lifetime? Washington, Lincoln, FDR, and possibly Reagan ("Tear down this wall Mr. Gorbachev") come to mind. Yet what about all the others? While it's tempting to place blame on the character or personality of modern presidents for their lack of accomplishment in some cases, it's important to take note of the fact that we have a divided system of government designed for the eighteenth century that we are trying to overlay on the complexities of the twenty-first century. Can a divided system of government make it possible to deal with such issues as a global financial meltdown, climate change, plagues, or holy wars?

To deliver on your mandate once in office, you may need to deal effectively with a divided system of government or other structural constraints.

Today, political scientists and economists have referred to our time as the "Chinese Century." China's leaders come into office with the power to reach high goals and solve complex problems with tremendous velocity due to a unified system of government that, despite its limitations with respect to democracy, has proven to be highly effective. Chinese leaders can set goals that amount to an Impossible Future and make unilateral decisions that result in transformational change without having to go through checks and balances. Mao transformed China from a backward medieval country that had been humiliated by foreign powers, into a modern superpower. Deng Zhao Peng declared a new era of capitalism with Chinese characteristics, and in less than thirty years, a billion people have been brought out of poverty.

You don't have to be the President of the United States or a cabinet official to feel the pressure that a divided system of government can bring, forcing you to reduce your vision of building an Impossible Future and rendering you incapable of bringing about transformational change. We hire very smart CEOs to run our big corporations, yet they often find themselves hamstrung in their first 100 days due to activist boards, Wall Street demands for short-term earnings, and/or divisions amongst the executive committee. At the same time, leaders at every level often find themselves tied up in knots due to excessive layers of bureaucratic rigmarole and hierarchy that seem to defy the individuals' ability to act powerfully in the face of their goals.

The chances are that if you are a newly installed leader, you are going to experience the same kind of frustrations well before your first 100 days are up. So what do you do? You can try to lead a revolution to bring about constitutional change or shift corporate culture but, in most cases, that is a hard road to follow. It's more realistic perhaps to enquire into how you can get more power and velocity in reaching your goals by tweaking the structure of your own organization and the culture that goes with it.

Does the Organization Structure Support Reaching Your Goals

- Do you have too many or too few people reporting to you?
- Are there too many layers of hierarchy?
- Which ones can be consolidated?
- Does the organization structure favor different department heads, just optimizing their part (giving rise to fiefdoms and kingdoms), or does it favor optimizing how the different parts interact?

THE PATH TO POWER

> *Power is the velocity with which*
> *you reach your goals.*

The whole point of this chapter is that you can use your charisma, talent, vote, connections, and campaign skills to get elected or hired to a powerful position, but this only represents the first milestone on the path to power. You have climbed and reached K2, the base camp for making the final assault on Mt Everest, but there is still a long way to go on the path to power. I am speaking of the path to gaining the power you will need in order to reach your goals and objectives once hired or in office. As mentioned earlier in this chapter, many leaders get close to the top of an organization, only to discover that they don't have the power necessary to accomplish what it is they need to accomplish with the velocity that is actually required.

Let's take for example the fact that all presidents of the last 30 years— Carter, Reagan, Bush I, Clinton, Bush II, and Obama—have declared a goal of peace in the Middle East, energy independence from foreign oil, and a high growth but green economy. But few Presidents have been able to mount the power to accomplish these goals with enough velocity to make a dent in the situation and, in most cases, their time in office is up before they can do something significant.

In the corporation, a newly installed CEO (or executive) has the positional power to hire and fire, pull off mergers and acquisitions, and to cut costs. Yet few CEOs or executives are able to marshal enough power to reach an Impossible Future, like coming up with innovative products that result in double digit organic growth, pulling off a major change initiative like Six Sigma quality, or transforming corporate culture, at least in this lifetime. The fact is that in most firms, while there is no shortage of brilliant change initiatives presented to the executive committee on a monthly basis, most of these ideas never actually come to pass due to the fact that the champion cannot find the path to power before the clock runs out and it's no longer relevant.

While a person's power is usually associated with the position they hold, this kind of power is only enough to get you on the chessboard with the ability to take some kind of action. Yet most leaders find that this kind of position-based power is insufficient to allow them to take a vision or intended change and actually bring it to pass. I would like to define "power" here not just in terms of your ability to accomplish a goal or objective that looks larger than yourself, but also in terms of the velocity in which you achieve it. Power is the velocity with which you can accomplish your goals.

> *Great leaders in government find the*
> *path to power by energizing their party*
> *and aligning their organization.*

If you stand for a big vision or big change, as James MacGregor Burns has pointed out, one thing is certain: you are going to be hated. FDR took that in stride when he accepted the nomination for the Democratic presidential candidate in 1932 in the middle of the Great Depression. He talked about all the people who hated him and all he stood for with his New Deal and then thundered aloud at Madison Square Garden, "I welcome their hatred." He took his campaign to the air and to the streets, demonstrating his love of the American people by talking about the suffering of people in breadlines and soup kitchens. The hatred that his opponents expressed against him soon only began to reflect their own pettiness, selfishness, and greed.

Generate a Tidal Wave of Support

One thing is clear both in politics and in business, great leaders with visions of an Impossible Future know that they must generate a tidal wave of political support to overcome the tidal wave of political opposition. That's why great presidents like FDR or Ronald Reagan are great believers in strong parties, why great CEOs like Jack Welch, are great believers in strongly aligned executive teams, as well as creating alignment with people at every level in the organization, and why revolutionaries like Mao are great believers in strong insurgencies.

FDR had tremendous personal charisma and the ability to bring brilliant men and women together to advise him. Yet FDR did not rely merely on his inner circle to help him find the path to power either before or after his election. He not only took his case for the New Deal to the American people, but also spent a great deal of time and effort energizing his party. He campaigned for his New Deal and ran for office on his own behalf and on behalf of many other Democratic party candidates who responded in kind by campaigning for him.

FDR's speeches (a chicken in every pot) gave leaders at every level of the Democratic Party not just a vision but also a place to stand in the sun against their opponents who seemed to stand in darkness. When FDR was elected, he brought many senators and congressman in on his coattails (at the national and state level). As a result, he was able to pass sweeping reforms from his very first days in office.

James MacGregor Burns points out in his book *Running Alone* that more recent presidents such as JFK, Jimmy Carter, and Bill Clinton tended to run alone, neither expecting much support from Democratic Party candidates nor offering much support to Democratic Party candidates in return. They may have had the personal charisma to attract millions of voters and to build their own well-heeled campaign organization, but when they got elected, they found that they were alone and without the power necessary to govern. Instead of reaching out to the people who ushered them into office or the party, they tended to reach back into their inner circle, often with disastrous consequences.[22]

Thus the path to power for any newly elected president or politician is to articulate a vision of an Impossible Future based on enduring human needs, to heal divisions within the party that make it dysfunctional, and to reach out to party members at all levels. It is my belief that the only way for a President to realize their Impossible Future in a divided system of government, is to transform their party from a loose political affiliation "I am for the little guy" or "I hate big government" into a viable change insurgency with the power to bring about sweeping reforms. You need party leaders at all levels who can talk up the Impossible Future, offer up good candidates, coach people in effective campaigning, drive legislation, and all the while stay connected with the people.

Barack Obama bypassed the standard party route and using the new digital media created a change insurgency which got him elected. Millions came to his website to donate money and read messages that told them where and when to show up at rallies. Since being elected, President Obama has continued to rely on his digital Democratic party change insurgency and successfully passed his health care bill and banking bill. Having said that, whether President Obama continues to be effective in bringing about change and being re-elected will largely depend on his ability to tap into the older members of the Democratic party who know how to get things done.

BUSINESS EXECUTIVES FIND THE PATH TO POWER BY CREATING CHANGE INSURGENCIES

Executives in every company intuitively know that, regardless of the brilliance of their Impossible Future and change programs, the power to realize them lies in creating alignment. In most cases, a tremendous amount of energy is spent on aligning the CEO and executive committee, which makes a certain amount of sense, given that most corporations are hierarchical. The problem I have with this approach, however, is that it can leave your whole dream hinging on the vote of a cantankerous CEO or an executive committee member who just doesn't get it.

So that they don't become discouraged, I often suggest to my coaching clients a two-headed approach to this dilemma. On one level, you can *play their game*, paying homage to the CEO and executive committee by taking your Impossible Future and change initiatives through the formal approval process or by putting aside your agenda for a while and focusing on how to help the CEO and others achieve their agenda. As one high-level Pentagon executive told me, the key to getting top-down power in any big organization is to become one of the "inner circle," or as he put it, one of the "depended upons" who the guy at the top can go to for a powerful assist on any number of things.

In order to be one of the "depended upons," you have to first of all be likeable and have some of the characteristics of a servant leader who wants the boss, as well as others, to succeed. Secondly, you need some expertise in a vital area of the business. You have to work very hard and you have to be able to sort through complex issues and add value on a consistent basis. If you do this, you will increase your level of standing and can leverage your position to wheel and deal with higher ups. If for example you are asked to clean up a messy operation, you may be able to say, "I will do this for you, if you do support my Impossible Future project"—or give me a promotion or a raise in pay.

On another level, you can *play your game* and start what I call a change insurgency. We live in a world where the "Chiefs" (the CEO, CFO, and CIO) of old-line companies cannot possibly know all the sudden shifts in technologies, new marketing trends, or customers' preferences. In a world of constant change, your job is not just to follow the orders of those at the top of the political chessboard; your job is to create change. Yet to bring about change, you have to learn to become not just a "change agent" officially appointed by those at the top, but also a "change insurgent" who sees an opportunity to make a difference, and seizes it.

Focus on What You Can Do Today

Change insurgency doesn't depend on formal rank, but rather on great ideas, powerful visions, and daring examples. If you work in a company like Google, which encourages people to use imagination and innovation, that's great. Otherwise, you have to "build your own sandbox," said one change insurgent I talked to in a big company. You have to seek out and work with people who are switched on by your Impossible Future and transformational agenda and try to spread the enthusiasm for what you are up to from that core. The key is to focus not just on what might be done, if you had all the power and resources you wish for, but also on what can be done today. Start with paying attention to what's missing that can make a difference and devise some catalytic breakthrough projects that will give you some quick wins and create the opening for larger change.

> *You don't have to be at the top to create change;*
> *you can create change from wherever you are.*

Sometimes there are enough people at the top, middle, and bottom who want to change with you; and sometimes you can do that within the formal organization. If that's the case, you can use your insurgency to turn up the heat by getting people to talk it up or by providing PowerPoints about your goals and plans, and using Facebook connections to build your network, YouTube videos to get your message out, and Twitter to show progress. If you do this, you may find that your idea goes viral and you start to receive both tangible and intangible support for your next catalytic breakthrough project from unexpected places.

At other times, you need to build a wall between your group and the rest of the company until you get big enough support and have enough strength to hold your own and to impress the rest of the organization.

YOU MAY NEED TO BE BOTH THE *LION* AND THE *FOX*

The ability of a president to master both houses of Congress or a business executive to get the buy in of the executive team (to borrow a phrase from Machiavelli) depends on being both the lion and the fox. You need to have the strength of a lion to stand for your idea amid opposition and to fight off wolves attacking from all sides, as well as to embody personal virtues, such as honesty, integrity, and keeping one's word. Yet, Machiavelli also points out that a prince needs to be like a fox to win the king's favor and to avoid getting caught up in snares.

As a newly installed executive, you must not only have the determination of a lion to pursue your Impossible Future against all odds, but also use the cunning of the fox to get the CEO and others to think it's their idea, embellish it with a strong business case, and make it appear that the change you are trying to bring about is something less akin to a revolution than an evolution. Whereas the lion must persevere in taking a stand for the Impossible Future and never giving up, the fox must figure out the unwritten rules of the game in order to proceed.

Understand the Unwritten Rules of the Game

- What kind of people does the CEO like?

- What do you do to get noticed in a favorable light?

- Who has real power on the executive team and who doesn't?

- How do the interests of the people on the executive team vary?

- Who are the fair-minded colleagues you can trust? Who are the sharks?

- How do you present new ideas (proposals) to the CEO and executive committee in a way that they will get supported?

- What is the way things work around here and what are the forces they generate? How can you harness those forces to get to your goals?

- What attitudes or behaviors will unwittingly get you into trouble? Who can mentor you?

YOUR 100 DAY GAME PLAN AND GRAND POLITICAL STRATEGY

The genius of leadership lies in the manner in which leaders visualize, care about, and act on their followers' aspirations and motivations.

The following are some suggestions that will get you on the right track for mastering the political chessboard from day one. As you will recall, we offered a way to map the political chessboard with all its shifting power grids and conflicting interests. Use that to make decisions on the following actions.

1) **Set up your first speech and first town hall meetings with your group.** In the United States and other countries, all new presidents begin their time in office with an inaugural address or in the UK as making one's "Maiden Speech." Jack Welch made his first speech as CEO of GE the day he got the job, saying GE would be #1 or #2 in every business. Use your first speech as a way to sound the tone that there is a new leader in town and to signal a shift in the wind. Frame your speech in a way that will resonate for people and "speak to their listening".

2) **Build your leadership capital and unite a divided organization in a common cause by dealing with crisis.** A great crisis is one of the ways a leader can establish his or her credibility, as well as unite a divided system of government or organization in a common cause. It is important to directly and proactively deal with the crisis once it surfaces, rather than seek to minimize its importance or delay intervention. Act like you are onstage in a crisis, because you are. People will be watching to see if your intervention is both proactive and sufficient.

> *Be a transactional leader who gets*
> *things done by wheeling and dealing and*
> *establishing a track record of success.*

3) **Focus the first half of your first hundred days, not on what *might* be done, but on what *can* be done.** Make sure that when you take on your new role that you are clear on your Day Job, get your house in order, and start to deliver on expectations. In his first hundred days, FDR wheeled and dealed with members in both Houses of Congress to pass a slew of legislation, most of which was remedial in nature. He used his ability as a *transactional leader* to get things done, cutting deals and linking different power bases. This allowed him to eventually pass *transformational* legislation that would represent historic change.

4) **Focus the second half of your first 100 days on building alignment around your Impossible Future and winning game plan.** Create a Source Document or the vision, goals, and ideas that you shared with others in your first 100 days will disappear. A Source Document is an artifact that puts your vision, goals, guiding principles and methodologies in one place. It gives you and everyone else in your organization a place to stand and is a tool for creating alignment. It should be based on an inspiring vision and empowering values that arouse people's aspirations and lift them to become their better selves.

Elements of a Source Document

- Your Impossible Future or transformational agenda, consistent with enduring human needs
- Your: a) vision, b) major goals and milestones, c) guiding principles and methodologies
- Iterate! Written in inspiring language that arouses people's aspirations and motivations
- Put the message out to all people in your organization in one-on-one conversations, small meetings, or larger town hall meetings

GUIDING PRINCIPLES AND PRACTICES

1) **The leader who is most likeable wins!** One of the best pieces of advice I can offer is to get some 360 feedback in your first 100 days from friends and colleagues about just how likeable you are. If you have some things to work on, like being abrasive, not listening, or being stiff, find a coach or mentor who can help you with them.

2) **Great leaders have great empathy.** At the core of all great political leadership is the ability to empathize with the throbbing human needs and wants. Abraham Lincoln would often stay up late at night grieving about the lives of fallen soldiers who were just boys. Bill Clinton connected with voters when he said, "I feel your pain." In your first 100 days, meet with people to find out about the issues that are really on their minds.

3) **Visualize an Impossible Future that arouses people's aspirations and becomes a rallying cry.** Think FDR's "A chicken in every pot;" Martin Luther King's, "I have a dream;" Steve Jobs of Apple, "We are going to change the world with the personal computer." By contrast, the goals and objectives of most business leaders are duller than the finish on an old truck and seldom inspire anyone to get in and go for a ride with you.

4) **Don't get stuck in dead center.** President Bill Clinton was a master politician who had a bold vision when he came into office. He began by taking a liberal, Democratic stand for a national healthcare bill, but when he got shot down by Congress over that, he retreated to dead center. Instead of offering up a legislative agenda based on his vision and values, he offered one based on what would pass muster with opinion polls and the press. Although President Clinton is still very popular, it would be hard for most to recall his single greatest accomplishment.

5) Find political advisors, campaign operatives, and a coach or confidant. Every presidential candidate has recognized that it is all too easy to get blindsided and crushed by political forces you didn't know were there. As such, all presidents seek political advisors, operatives, and coaches who can give them a broader and deeper view of the political landscape and help them plot campaign strategies, win people over, and untangle situations. Business executives, university presidents, heads of state, and hospital directors with big goals should do the same.

6) The art of the deal. *Transactional leadership* involves one leader or group exchanging something with another leader or group without any further commitment or loyalty being granted. You don't have to love them or be ideologically compatible; you just have to find a basis for making tradeoffs that will be mutually beneficial. Think about what you want to accomplish in your first 100 days and beyond and also the missing pieces that need to be put in place. What friends or foes can you practice the "art of the deal" with to get one of those missing pieces?

7) Build coalitions of unlikely collaborators to get things done. Many executives and elected officials come to power by focusing on a narrow base of support. President George W. Bush focused on right wing Republicans and Bill Clinton on liberal Democrats. This can get you elected, but it is not sufficient to get your agenda accepted. In order to do that, you need to *broaden the base.* For example, President Barack Obama found unexpected support for his Immigration bill in right wing Republican evangelical ministers, especially those whose congregations were heavily Hispanic.

8) It's not personal, it's business. One of my favorite stories concerns President Ronald Reagan and House Speaker Tip O'Neill. The two were on opposite sides of the issue almost all the time by day, yet when night rolled around, President Reagan would often invite speaker O'Neill to the

White House to drink scotch, play cards, and tell jokes and stories, thus keeping their relationship whole. When President Reagan would ask for O'Neill for support on this or that bill, O'Neill would say, "Mr. President that bill is never going to pass." He would always then add that, if the President compromised on this or that, the Speaker might be able to get enough votes to get it through. The two counted each other as "great friends."

9) The next election or CEO review is never far away, so be ready to crow about your accomplishments. Executives who take stands and accomplish a great deal in their first 100 days and after will inevitably create opposition and take their knocks in the court of public opinion. As accomplishments tend to disappear, where mistakes live on in infamy, it is very important to keep in mind that the next election or executive review is never far away, and in order to do well, you have to be prepared to trot out your list of accomplishments and crow about yourself. Think backward from your vision, list what you want to accomplish, and create a scoreboard that tells you in dollars and cents and other tangible measures just how much you have really achieved.

SUMMARY

- Getting to the top is not enough; to realize an Impossible Future and succeed in your Day Job, you must master the political chessboard.
- Spend sufficient time talking to people to understand the nature of political chessboard that you exist on.
- Map out the political chessboard in terms of *supporters, opposers, neutrals.* Ask: *Who are the key players, their unseen advisors, and confidants?*
- Look at what you need to do to build support, overcome opposition, and bring people to your side.

- Build coalitions to accomplish what you want to accomplish; *master the art* of the deal by focusing on shared interests versus positions.
- Be a "lion," with the strength to a stand for your ideas amid opposition and fight off attacks; be a "fox" with the cunning to win favor and avoid getting caught up in snares.

CHAPTER 8

LAUNCH 90-DAY CATALYTIC BREAKTHROUGH PROJECTS

Build Confidence and Credibility Through Quick Wins

EVERY YEAR THOUSANDS of managers make transitions into new jobs. The actions that they and other new leaders take during their first few months have a big impact on their success or failure. From 1999 to 2006, the average tenure of departing chief executive officers in the United States dropped from about 10 years to about 8 years. Although some CEOs stay over three years, a lot of them find that their duty in the corner office is surprisingly short. In 2006, for instance, about forty percent of CEOs who lost jobs had lasted an average of just 1.8 years, according to a study by the outplacement firm Challenger, Gray & Christmas. Survival for the lower half of this group was only eight months.

They were ushered out the door because they appeared unable to improve the business's performance. Nobody these days gets much time to show what he or she can do. So within the first 100 days at most, incoming CEOs and general managers must zero in on ways to increase market share, overtake competitors, and impact profitability—whatever the key tasks may be. However, they can't map out specific objectives and initiatives until they know where they are starting from which is why the due diligence period is so important.

It's important to note that executive transitions are also times when organizations can be transformed, in part because everybody is expecting a big change. However, the first 100 days is the time when new leaders are also most vulnerable, because they lack detailed knowledge of the new role and haven't established new working relationships. So what does it take to make a successful transition?

In the Harvard Business Review I came across a study done a few years ago that provided some crucial insight to this question. The study was done in cooperation with the Corporate Executive Board's Learning and Development Roundtable—a group of executives, mainly from large firms responsible for cultivating leadership talent—who sponsored the research project to find out the key to successful executive transitions. The idea was to search for clues as to what distinguished the executives who were succeeding in their new jobs from those who were struggling.

One attribute stood out among the high-performing new leaders: a strong focus on results. In fact, most had figured out how to gain an early success or "quick win" – a new and visible contribution to the most important goals and objectives of the business made within the first few months of their taking the job. Those who had achieved a quick win scored on average nearly 20 percent higher than those who hadn't.

This was an interesting finding, underlining the importance of newly promoted executives' need to put points on the board fast. A quick win is a strong form of reassurance: a) to the executive's bosses, who want to believe they have made the right promotion decision, b) to colleagues on the leadership team seeking to judge whether a real player has joined their ranks, and c) to direct reports deciding whether to place confidence in their new boss.[23]

PITFALLS FOR LEADERS IN A NEW JOB

The study also pointed out some interesting things about leaders who struggled in their new jobs, which may be instructive to you.

1) **Getting bogged down in their vision by making elaborate plans and preparations.** An Impossible Future can sound good on paper, but people can easily get bogged down in the discouraging complexity of trying to mount a big change initiative in an organization that may not be ready for it.

2) **Putting too much attention on pie-in-the-sky goals, not enough on doing their Day Job.** I have found that coaching new executives is about helping them maintain a delicate balance between stepping out onto the limb on an Impossible Future and making sure they deliver on the basics that everyone expects.

3) **Focusing too much on criticism from bosses and colleagues.** New executives may be hired with a going-in mandate that represents change, but then meet criticism when they actually pursue it. Instead of seeking a path forward, they often lash out, head for the bunkers, or obsess about criticism.

4) **Jumping to conclusions.** New executives in a role, like Head of Marketing or Head of Engineering, often come with old preconceptions from previous assignments about how to be successful that may cause them to jump to conclusions about fundamental causes and solutions. These preconceptions can cause them to filter out contrary information or prevent them from really listening to their team. They may also be prone to lecture their team with their views rather than draw people out for input on the real situation.

5) **Getting down in the weeds.** Imagine the insecurity a person might feel in becoming President of the United States (or president of a large corporation) and finding themselves in a far more complex job than they had imagined. Some chief executives, like United States President Jimmy

Carter, tried to deal with this insecurity by focusing too much on details. The same thing happens to many executives in a big new assignment.

Clearly one of the antidotes to many of the leadership ills mentioned above is to focus on catalytic breakthrough projects or quick wins.

Setting Up a Catalytic Breakthrough Project:

1) Cuts down on overly elaborate planning and preparations
2) Creates a focus on breakthrough goals that are neither too big nor too small
3) Prevents jumping to conclusions by engaging the views and perspectives of the team
4) Determines what can be done with existing resources and authority
5) Creates a path forward that will help to get buy-in.

CATALYTIC BREAKTHROUGH PROJECTS TO SPEARHEAD A BREAKTHROUGH

As my coaching work is about helping executives realize an Impossible Future, I often find myself helping executives jump start their goals with something I have called a 90-day catalytic breakthrough project. The idea here is to launch a small, high-leverage project to spearhead a breakthrough that, if successful, will in turn create the opening for a larger breakthrough.

For example, I met a young executive in Shanghai from Zara, the Spanish high fashion retail chain, who was tasked with business development in emerging markets in twelve countries. One 90-day catalytic breakthrough project was to get close to the market in one country, and understand customers' habits, tastes, and price points. A second was to open one store in one country that showed immediate signs of being a smashing success.

It is important to connect the catalytic breakthrough project to an Impossible Future, with the idea of getting some points up on the scoreboard quickly. For example, an oil refinery manager we coached decided to go for a quick win that involved three lost profit opportunities in their oil refinery, having to do with a) speeding up shutdown time for annual repairs, b) increasing energy utilization in running the refinery, and c) less wait time at fueling stations for customers with trucks.

I also coached his boss on a catalytic breakthrough project, which had to do with training eighteen managers to become Six Sigma Blackbelts tied into launching a quality revolution in the company. Each Blackbelt had to teach others to start Six Sigma projects that would eliminate lost profit opportunities. This was the first time a Six Sigma program (a process closely associated with General Electric) had been tried in the oil industry. This catalytic breakthrough project was a small breakthrough that led to a much larger breakthrough. It directly resulted in training many more Black Belts, initiating hundreds of Six Sigma projects, and savings of billions of dollars.

WHAT IS A CATALYTIC BREAKTHROUGH PROJECT?

I use the catalytic breakthrough projects in my coaching work, as mentioned above, to help clients jump start their Impossible Future rather than get bogged down by the elaborate planning and preparations or get caught in the discouraging complexity of trying to bring about major change in an organization. There is also the issue that, in addition to the Impossible Future, my clients usually have a lot on their plates already with their Day Job and may find it difficult to find the time to make a D-Day type assault on the beachheads that would make their vision a reality. As Tony Jimenez from Chevron Texaco once suggested to me, the Impossible Future is like a big ball of twine that is all tangled up. All you need to unravel is a place to start, and the catalytic breakthrough project gives you a great way to do that.

What do we mean by "Catalytic"?

The definition of catalytic in chemistry is "a substance, usually used in small amounts relative to the reactants, that modifies and increases the rate of a reaction without being consumed in the process." In the context we are using it, catalytic means that it is a small project relative to the Impossible Future that, if achieved, modifies the possibility of actually reaching the Impossible Future, while adding power and velocity to the process.

For example, in the decade leading up to the American rebellion from the British empire, there was a lot of talk about big ideas like democracy, freedom from tyranny, human rights and so on. Yet for the most part it remained talk (hot air) and didn't gain enough force to actually make anything happen.

An inspired individual named Thomas Paine offered up his own version of a catalytic breakthrough project when he published his pamphlet "Common Sense," by far the most influential tract of the American Revolution. Paine's political pamphlet brought the rising revolutionary sentiment into sharp focus by placing blame for the suffering of the colonies directly on the reigning British monarch, George III. First and foremost, Common Sense advocated an immediate declaration of independence, postulating a special moral obligation of America to the rest of the world. Not long after publication, the spirit of Paine's argument found resonance in the American Declaration of Independence and led to the war for independence, as well as the USA Constitution that was to shape, limit, and define the American nation.

Throughout history, you will see many examples where catalytic breakthrough projects have helped or would have helped realize an Impossible Future, had they been used by new leaders in their first hundred days. For example, Franklin Delano Roosevelt (FDR) launched a blizzard of catalytic "make work" programs like the Civilian Conservation Core (CCC) designed to get America out of the Great Depression. These programs were short-lived, but they paved the way for what FDR called an Economic Bill of Rights for All Americans, which led to long-term programs social security, unemployment compensation, and Medicare. FDR recognized the need for a universal health care bill, but stopped short of pushing for it, as he thought the country didn't have the political or economic will to make it happen.

Interestingly enough, Bill Clinton tried to push a big healthcare bill through in his first hundred days and later President Barack Obama followed suit during the early days of his Presidency. Had President Clinton initiated a catalytic breakthrough project rather than trying to push his healthcare bill through as a complete package, he might have succeeded. Newt Gingrich, Speaker of the House at that time, said after the bill failed, that if Hillary Clinton, who was in charge of this bill, had brought twenty percent of the bill through that first year, they would have passed it and she would have gained some momentum. The next year she could have brought another twenty percent and they would have passed that and the momentum would have increased. And the third year, twenty more.

What do we mean by "Breakthrough"?

The word "breakthrough" is defined in the dictionary in four ways, and each is relevant to us here:
1. A productive insight
2. Making an important discovery
3. A penetration of a barrier that has prevented progress
4. An extraordinary result

If you think of people like Thomas Edison in his lab working on the invention of the light bulb, Henry Ford working on the first assembly line, or Watson and Crick working on the first DNA double helix model, each of the four elements of the above definition of a breakthrough would apply. However, there is perhaps one missing element to this definition, and that is that most breakthroughs are not discovered while sitting under a tree, like Isaac Newton dreaming about the law of gravity. Most often, they are discovered in the process of taking action in the context of a live project aimed at an extraordinary result.

A catalytic breakthrough project needs to be aimed at a small but extraordinary and tangible result that, if achieved, will create the opening for an even greater result. Steve Jobs had a dream of changing the world with the personal computer and started a breakthrough project in his garage that involved an extraordinary and tangible result – building the first Apple personal computer. This project was catalytic in that, before this time, computers were either big heavy pieces of equipment that usually filled special air-conditioned rooms in large corporations, or a mini-computer kit that the consumer had to put together, or a portable computer made by IBM with a price tag of $10,000 that only business or educational institutions could afford.

Another example is Bill Gates, who had a vision of creating a great company that would come to fame by controlling the software inside the computers. His catalytic breakthrough project was aimed at an extraordinary result – that of selling IBM executives (the company that was at that time the colossus of the computer business) on adopting Microsoft operating system rather than going with their own in-house operating system. At the time he made his proposal, the early version of Microsoft's operating system was more or less a work in progress, far from a finished product. As soon as Gates closed the deal with IBM, he had to start another 90-day catalytic breakthrough project with a small team to actually build the software. Today, Microsoft is a company that has a market cap something like a 1000 times great than IBM.

KEY CRITERIA FOR CATALYTIC BREAKTHROUGH PROJECTS

Each of these conditions is very important and must not be overlooked in formulating a catalytic breakthrough project.

1. It jump starts your Impossible Future. The idea is to bypass elaborate planning and preparations or getting discouraged by the complexity of the situation by mounting a small project and going for a result now.

2. It is a small, high-leverage project that is aimed at spearheading a breakthrough result that will create the opening for a larger breakthrough. The idea is to mount a small breakthrough project aimed at an extraordinary and tangible result that, if achieved, will create an opening for a higher order of results. Even catalytic breakthrough projects with limited results often lead to powerful insights and important discoveries, or they help penetrate barriers.

3. It is aimed at a focused goal that can only be achieved with imaginative thinking and innovative action. Catalytic breakthrough projects are aimed at an extraordinary result that has the potential to change everything, not just to lead to continuous improvement. For example, I worked with a company that came up with a new carbon fiber technology. One of the first steps was to build a pilot plant that showed it could be manufactured en masse.

4. It is inclusive: Who wants to play? One of the things you want to establish in your first hundred days is that you are not a dead hero, but a team player. A catalytic breakthrough project is a good way to get colleagues and direct reports involved.

5. It is a dream with a deadline! It can be accomplished in under 90 days. It's been pointed out by Robert Schaeffer author of "The Breakthrough Strategy" that teams come together around a project when there are razor sharp goals and success is near and clear.[24]

Examples of Catalytic Breakthrough Projects

- Phase 1 of a big project that's a great first step
- Pilot projects or pilot anything before scaling up
- Experimenting with a new (material) method like Six Sigma in one department
- Collaborating with customers on a product with game-changing potential
- Designing a micro website in advance of the product
- Creating a YouTube video to make your idea go viral
- Entering an emerging market through one retail store
- Giving your top ten high-potential leaders a transformational assignment
- Outsourcing one department—for example the transactional area of the HR department
- Using one recycled "green material" in your manufacturing process

Three Notes of Caution

I have seen some coaches and coachees who have struggled with taking their Impossible Future and formulating a catalytic breakthrough project. So pay attention to the following:

- The goals of the catalytic breakthrough projects must not be too big, or too small
- The project must be framed to achieve a result that will take you to a different place, not just geared toward continuous improvement.
- You need to personally get involved vs. delegate the catalytic breakthrough projects to your team

You make big decisions aimed at "doing the impossible" when you are in a position of power and high leverage. You go for small quick wins aimed at "doing the obvious" when you are part of a leadership coalition or don't have a proper mandate.

Target Some Catalytic Breakthrough Projects

Identify 1 to 3 quick wins and score each on a scale of 1 to 20 according to the following criteria:

- **Connection to business results:** Is the quick-win targeted to meaningful business outcomes with a clear connection to revenue or cost reduction? If successful, will it attract the attention of managers two levels above?
- **Cost and feasibility:** Can this quick-win be achieved with existing resources and authority, and not distract the team too much from its daily job?
- **Opportunity to engage:** Will this quick-win give me the opportunity to engage with bosses and colleagues at other levels of the organization? Will it give me the opportunity to coach, guide, and seek input from direct reports?
- **Learning opportunity:** Will pursuing this quick-win give me an opportunity to learn? Will it allow me to learn about the aspirations, motivations, strengths and weaknesses of my team?
- **Shared credit:** Will key members of the team be able to see their fingerprints on the quick win? Will they get credit? Is there plenty of opportunity for them to play?

SUMMARY

- Energize people and get them focused on cracking important business problems in ways that will have an immediate and dramatic impact by the end of the 100 days.
- Look at your Impossible Future and your Day Job and find a place where you can do a 90-day (30 or 60 day) catalytic breakthrough project that will spearhead a breakthrough.
- Don't get bogged down in elaborate planning and preparation, but do identify a high opportunity area (and only one) where early wins are probable: *marketing, new product development, sales, costs.*
- The idea is to find a place that, if you succeed, it brings you to a different place and you see new openings for a larger breakthrough.
- Go where there is existing readiness and where you have the authority, resources and support to make something quickly happen.
- Focus on not just the "what," but "how" quick wins are achieved.
- Create pilot projects that not only produce results but also fosters people on the team thinking and interacting together according to your vision of how the organization should work.

CHAPTER 9

EXECUTIVE TIME MANAGEMENT

Focus on Making a Difference, Not the Important

DID YOU EVER see the movie Inception, a movie about dreams? In the movie, the main character, Leonardo DiCaprio, asks his protégé: "Do you know if you are dreaming now or awake? If it is a dream, you don't know how you got here, or how you will leave." So here you are, just a number of days into your new executive assignment wanting to schedule a meeting with an important colleague about either your Impossible Future or your Day Job—and you discover that you don't have a single opening on your calendar for a month. You might wonder how did I wind up here? How will I possibly escape?

A few days later, you find yourself sitting in your office at 6:30 pm about to head out but bewildered by the fact that you are leaving behind a trail of unfinished tasks and unanswered phone calls and emails. As you pack up to leave, you are haunted by the feelings of guilt that it is already late and you may miss dinner again tonight with your family. On some level, you know that you have lost control of your time—*and your life*—but you don't know what to do about it.

*You ask yourself, "How is it that I am
already falling into a black hole of time
management? How did this happen?"*

Most executives begin a new assignment ready to spread their wings and fly high, but then fall into a kind of black hole of time management. How did this happen? First there are the demands of the corporate calendar – formal budget reviews, operations reviews, and people reviews that take up huge chunks of time. Then there are dozens of daily telephone calls, hundreds of emails and endless meetings. It's all quite a mind-numbing experience.

*The first 100 days is a chance to plan
how much time you will spend on
your Impossible Future and how much
you will spend on your Day Job.*

Don't Let the "Urgent" Crowd Out the "Important"

Back in the 1960s, Charles Hummel, a minister (management consultant of the day) was touring a cotton mill. He asked the manager what were two of the greatest lessons he had learned in 30 years on the job. The manager said that the first was to set some clear goals and priorities. The second was to make sure that the urgent didn't crowd out the important. The cotton mill manager's answers provide a lot of insight for most executives who have fallen into the black hole of "mis-time-management."

In Hummel's classic essay "Tyranny of the Urgent," written in 1967, he identified things such as the telephone ringing (especially if the call is from the boss checking up on things) as among the worst offenders against our creativity and productivity. And that was before we carried the offending instrument with us everywhere and embellished it with email, computers, cameras, downloadable ringtones and music files.

If Hummel were an executive in his first 100 days in a big government agency or corporation today, his list of "worst offenders" of letting the "urgent" crowd out the "important" would have included:

- Your cell phone ringing every ten minutes
- 200 to 300 emails a day that demand a reply
- Weekly staff meetings that cause you to interrupt your brainwork
- Personnel review forms that are needed by noon
- A 5 PM plane to attend a corporate offsite in Utah
- Nightly dinners or charity events to attend
- The crisis du jour

Have you ever wished for a thirty-hour day? Surely this extra time would relieve the tremendous pressure under which an executive lives in their first 100 days. With a thirty-hour day, you may discover for a week or so that your days are less pressure packed. However, I would suspect that soon you would find yourself back in the black hole with no time to work on your real goals and leaving a trail of unfinished tasks behind you. And yes, haunted in the odd moment by the usual guilt about phone calls you didn't return, emails you didn't respond to, and family dinners you missed.

The Problem is Not Lack of Time, But One of Priorities

The point is that a thirty-hour day probably wouldn't solve your problem. The fact is that the real issue goes deeper than the shortage of time. The real problem is the lack of priorities. This is why we leave undone things that should have been done and do things we shouldn't have done. As Charles Hummel so brilliantly pointed out, the heart of the matter lies in the fact that our priorities often get distorted when we allow the "urgent" to crowd out the "important". How does this happen? The answer: 1) hierarchy, 2) peer pressure, and 3) random events.

How Priorities Get Distorted

1. One urgent call from the boss can make you forget your Impossible Future or even forget to do your Day Job. Imagine you are working on your Impossible Future presentation. You are in a state of deep concentration, about to move beyond the question at hand and arrive at the moment of true insight. You then get a phone call, the 28th hour of the day, which demands that you break your state of deep concentration, just at the moment when it was about to come to fruition. The last call you got was from your spouse asking you what you wanted for dinner. This call is from your boss, so you'd "better take it." He asks you to get involved in a goal or problem that involves cleaning up a mess, and pretty soon everything is a blur. By the next time you are able to get back to your Impossible Future presentation, three or four weeks have gone by. I am not suggesting that you not take the boss's phone call, or that you Ignore your boss in any way, but I am suggesting that you not lose sight of the whole picture and what you are trying to accomplish.

2. Peer pressure to attend meetings can unwittingly cause you to have no time left for your key goals or projects. Another example of things that lead to distortion of priorities is when we make the decision to put aside, for example, our big presentation to the board, the one that our entire game plan is riding on, and instead we attend a so-called urgent meeting called today by another department head. Upon arriving, we discover it really wasn't that urgent after all. Most executives in their first 100 days want to appear positive and upbeat, with a "can-do" attitude that causes them to say "yes" to everything. This, in turn, leads them to acquiesce to peer pressure and overcommit. The only solution is to recognize that while you have the *power to say yes* to peer pressure, you also have the *power to say no*.

Four Meeting Ground Rules to Better Manage Your Time

1. Set a timer and make sure the meeting ends on time

2. Have a clear agenda

3. Start the meeting with a specific problem

4. Make sure there are as few people at the meeting as possible

---

3. Random interruptions can destroy your productivity. Ask yourself, when do you get the most work done? If you are like most executives, it's at night or in the morning when there is no one else around. The rest of the day is full of interruptions that break your work day into a series of fleeting moments. It's eleven in the morning when you hear, "15 minutes and then you have a conference call." An hour later comes lunch, followed by an executive committee meeting. It's now three in the afternoon and your schedule is clear, a good time to go back to your pet project. You go to the coffee area and get a tap on the shoulder from a colleague, "Got a minute?" Before you know it, you look at the clock and it is six in the evening and you have only had one uninterrupted hour to get things done. It's great to collaborate, but if you want to accomplish things, you need to spend more time in the "alone zone". Set up one to two hours in the morning and early evening when you won't be interrupted. Work from home or the library.

Is there any escape? It's a fact of life that, as an executive in your first 100 days, you will have an incredible number of demands coming at you from the world around you. The key thing is to not confuse "urgent" demands coming at you from the *outside* with goals and top priorities that you yourself set from the *inside*. In the final analysis, you are accountable to both yourself and others for accomplishing what you need to accomplish. You need to be able to distinguish your real goals and priorities from the demands that are being hurled at you. Then you need to stick to your priorities, even if it's not easy. Here are some suggestions.

Stick to Your Priorities

1. Review your top priorities when you arrive and post them on your desk
2. Don't let "urgent" requests from your boss (and others) crowd out the "important"
3. Stop being a people pleaser in regards to meetings; develop the power to say "no"
4. Carve out your "alone zone" at home and at work so you are not interrupted

---

Most Forward Planning and Scheduling is Guesswork

Unless you are a fortune teller, long-term business planning, whether for your Impossible Future or Day Job, is sheer guesswork. There are just too many factors that you can't control — budget cuts, market conditions, customers' requests, competitors, the economy, and so on.

Authors Fried and Hansson of *Rework* say, "Why not then call *plans* what they really are: *guesses*."[25] Strategic plans are strategic guesses, financial plans are financial guesses. When you turn guesses into plans and plans into your time schedule, you enter a danger zone and begin to lose touch with reality. Further, most plans are driven by the past and thereby tend to put blinders on you. You may find yourself hacking your way through the jungle with a machete when there is a freeway ten yards to the left of you. The timing of most plans is messed up as well, because you get the most information while you are actually doing something, not before you do it.

Of course, it's a good idea to have an Impossible Future and winning game plan, but don't stress out over following it to the letter. You have to be prepared to improvise, to say, "We are going in this direction because this makes sense today." So give up on the idea of following a detailed plan and time schedule. Focus on what you are going to do this week versus what you are going to do this year. Pick the most important thing to do today and do it.

Think Backward From Your Vision and Then Jump Into Action

There is a saying with respect to realizing a vision "you can't get there from here, but you can get there from there." If you try to get there from here (forward planning), you tend to let the past determine the future. But if you try to get there from there (reverse planning), you let the future determine your actions. Stand in the future (either your Impossible Future or the practical objectives of your Day Job) as if it were already realized and ask yourself, "How did I get here?" Once you figure that out, you are ready to jump into action.

Stand in the future as if it were already realized and ask, how did I get here?

Stand in the Future and Plan From There

1. Imagine your Impossible Future or practical Day Job goals already realized.
2. What needed to happen for you to realize your vision?
3. How did you make it happen, regardless of difficult facts and circumstances?
4. What were the missing pieces that needed to be put in place in order to reach it? How did you come up with those missing pieces?
5. What were the key projects and tasks for those missing pieces?
6. What is a 90-day catalytic breakthrough project or quick win you can accomplish in weeks, not months?
7. Get going and produce some results right now, immediately.

THE FOUR QUADRANTS OF EXECUTIVE TIME MANAGEMENT

Most executives come up with an Impossible Future and then start out with a bang. They then begin struggling with finding time to work on their Impossible Future, their Day Job, on being a good team member, or even on personal renewal. It's a balancing act in any case, but one thing that can help is to divide your day (or week) according to The Four Quadrants of Executive Time Management. In Diagram 9.1 I suggest spending twenty-five percent of your day on your Impossible Future, twenty-five percent on your Day Job, twenty-five percent on the corporate calendar, and twenty-five percent on personal renewal.

Diagram 9.1 The Four Quadrants of Executive Time Management

25% Impossible Future	**25%** Day Job
25% Executive Team Member *corporate calendar*	**25%** Personal Renewel

You will discover that this is a very powerful rule of thumb, even if following it to the letter isn't always possible. If you don't have time to work on your Impossible Future today due to an all-day planning and budgeting session with the executive committee, you can always squeeze out a couple of extra hours in the morning or evening. If a three-day offsite prevents you from doing your Day Job this week or talking to your team, you can focus on that during the rest of the week, or call team members on your way to and from work.

Focus on the Most Important Things You Can Do Today and Do Them

One way to make sure you stick to the four quadrant technique is to divide your day into four key tasks every day. Make sure you do one thing every day in each category. It's important not to allow yourself any reasons or excuses, like "I don't have the time." It's always possible to squeeze out a couple of extra hours in any given day, if you train yourself to "keep the main thing the main thing." If you stick to the following, you will be amazed at how much you accomplish every day and how satisfying it is.

Divide Your Day According to the Four Quadrants

1. Choose the most important thing you can do on your Impossible Future today and do it
2. Choose the most important thing you can do on your Day Job today and do it
3. Choose the most important thing you can do to help someone else on the executive team today and do it
4. Choose the most important thing you can do to renew yourself today and do it

---

Focus on the Epicenter of Each Category

One question you may be asking yourself at this point is "How do I determine what is the most important thing I can do about my Impossible Future or Day Job today?" To be sure, there are 101 things you could probably think of doing in each of the quadrants, but again your time and attention is limited, so how do you prioritize? My suggestion is to focus on the epicenter, the one idea that lies at the center of all the other ideas you have. For example, let's say your Impossible Future is opening up a world famous hamburger restaurant. You can focus on all the décor, chairs and tables, condiments, and so on. Yet, if you want to have a world famous hamburger restaurant, the epicenter to focus on is a great tasting hamburger. Once you get that down, you can shift your focus to something else.

1. For my Impossible Future, the epicenter I need to focus on now is:
Let's say you have an idea for an Impossible Future to grow your business exponentially through a Blue Ocean Strategy that involves innovating products rather than trying to compete in the same old bloody Red Ocean on price. You can come up with many ideas to try to make this happen in your first 100 days, such as making a PowerPoint presentation, coming up with a clever brand marketing idea, designing a product, finding a customer, and so on. However, why not focus your time and attention on the one idea that lays at the epicenter of your Impossible Future, which is probably getting the buy-in of the board and the executive committee, without which your whole idea is a nonstarter. The usual approach is to come up with a document, which takes a long time and is easy to forget. I suggest other approaches that get people more involved. For example, sketching your idea with a marking pen, producing a video over the weekend, rapid prototyping of new products and services that will allow you to present your idea to those whose buy-in you must first gain.

2. For my Day Job, the epicenter I need to focus on is:
Let's say you are the CEO or head of marketing for a consumer goods company. Your Day Job roles include P&L responsibility, branding, advertising, channel distribution, and sales. What is the one aspect of your Day Job that lies at the epicenter, without which there wouldn't be a real reason for that Day Job, and that would be pivotal to desired results? Or you might

ask: What are the things that you could remove from your spectrum of roles and responsibilities without causing much of a stir? When Roberto Goizueta became CEO of Coca Cola, his goal was not increasing market share, but rather increasing "share of stomach." He spent much of his first 100 days talking to route drivers all over the country and encouraging them to get a Coke machine in every store and in every office building. He then focused on developing snack lines.

3. The epicenter of being a good team member (handling my corporate calendar) is:

One of your responsibilities as an executive in a company or government is to do what I call "own the whole game," not just your department. This means you have to be a good team member who places collective victory over individual glory. The epicenter of being a good team member, however, doesn't just involve going to every meeting on the corporate calendar; it also involves making the other people on the team successful. Peter Drucker, the great management guru, once remarked that the success of the British East India Company in the eighteenth and nineteenth century, despite its far-flung offices, was a direct result of people being trained to make good use of tools as simple as the quill pen and parchment paper. Each director of the British East India Company was trained to constantly ask themselves the question, "Who in the company needs encouragement, communication, and resources from me, and who do I need encouragement, communication, and resources from?"

4. The epicenter of renewing myself today is:

There are many things an individual executive like yourself does to get rid of stress and recharge your batteries. For example, spend some time having dinner with the family, eating healthy foods, going out for your daily walk or run, reading a good book, going to the movies, and getting a good night's sleep. Now ask yourself, what is the epicenter of that whole list? If you do that one thing, everything else falls into place; if you don't do it, everything falls apart. For example, for me getting a good night's sleep lies at the epicenter of personal renewal. I can go without good food or exercise for a while, but if I don't get a good night's sleep, you wind up behind the "eight ball" very fast. For example, if you are like most executives, you probably stubbornly press on and work longer hours on a big project, especially when you are faced with obstacles, even if you have to sacrifice sleep. Yet, have you ever noticed that one of the first things that goes when you are tired is the creativity needed to solve problems? The other thing that happens is that good humor, the kind that is necessary to deal with human conflicts, is usually replaced by irritability.

Exercise: How to avoid the black holes of executive time management.
I suggest doing this exercise with a coach or thinking partner on a monthly basis.

1. Write down a list of things that will keep you busy, but won't accomplish anything. For starters just think of the incredible number of demands coming at you vs. the demands of the corporate calendar: compulsory "boring" meetings, phone calls, frequent emails checks.

2. Write down a list of things you want to accomplish. Write down some of the things that, if you had the time, you would choose to do and that represent not only accomplishing what you really want to accomplish, but also the difference you want to make.

3. Schedule time to accomplish what you want to accomplish. Take out your calendar for the next three months and schedule from 30 to 70 percent of your time (a big chunk) on difference makers vs. busy maker activities. Just carve out some time and write it down.

4. Go back and review your calendar each month in reverse, analyzing every scheduled activity. Take your calendar from the previous month and mark every activity as either a "difference maker" or a "time waster". The goal is to get at least thirty to seventy percent of your time into the "difference maker" category.

THE TEN COMMANDMENTS OF TIME MANAGEMENT

You can avoid falling into the black hole of time management, if you follow these Ten Commandments:

1. Stop being a victim of your calendar.
The best way not to become a victim of your calendar is to reclaim it from other people. Take charge of and schedule your calendar as much as possible. Focus your time on things that will "make a difference" vs. things that are "trivial" or "important". Let your secretary keep you informed of requests for your time so that you can decide how you want to spend it.

2. Specifically schedule time on your Impossible Future; most of the rest will get scheduled automatically.
Most managers are inundated with the demands of the corporate calendar—planning and budgeting, business reviews, talent reviews. Not only do these items get scheduled automatically, but they are non-discretionary, which means you don't even have a choice as to whether or not to attend. What you do have a choice about is how you handle your discretionary time. I suggest that each week you consciously and intentionally schedule what you will do on Quadrant I. *Your Impossible Future.*

3. Focus on the part of your job where you have set transformational goals and, if possible, find a "number 2" to handle the transactional business.
I suggested to a senior vice president that I was coaching in their first 100 days to focus all their time on their Impossible Future, transformational stuff, and find a VP who was more of a nuts and bolts type to handle their Day Job and the transactional activities.

4. Accomplish quick wins to build rapid momentum.

Imagine how hard it would be to maintain your interest in watching a soccer game on TV that was going on for a year. In order for you (your team) to keep your head in the game, you need short-term goals where success is near and clear. Instead of launching a software program with all the bells and whistles this year, launch a key part of it and do so in the next two weeks. Then build on the momentum of the successes by launching another part as soon as it is completed. Instead of thinking of a 40-week project, think in terms of 40 one-week projects.

5. Spend time in the "Alone Zone".

As mentioned above, most people get the most done when they spend uninterrupted time alone working on projects they passionately care about. Start to consciously and intentionally build in time in the "alone zone" where you can get things done—early mornings or afternoons. Also brainstorm with your coach or confidant varied ways to make sure you are not interrupted while you are in it. 1) Alert your secretary that you are in the alone zone, 2) shut off your phone so you don't get calls, 3) work from home, the library, or the lounge at a five star hotel, 4) use email to collaborate vs. text messages and meetings.

6. Stop being a people pleaser. Just say "no" to mindless meetings. A

lot of people who work in big companies are people pleasers who have a hard time saying "no" to anything like a request to attend a meeting. Resolve to only attend meetings where your personal participation will make a difference. Just say "no" to meetings where your presence is symbolic.

7. Thou shalt get off the phone in no more than ten minutes and halt drive-by intrusions.

The truth is that with rare exception, most business phone calls don't have to last more than three minutes, yet most phone calls drone on for much longer. Ask at the beginning of the call: "What do we want to accomplish in this call?" Then see if you can get that done in 10 minutes, and 15 minutes at the maximum. Also, put a halt to drive-by meetings that can take up half your day. Here are a couple of tips: 1) Close your door and open it only when you are in the mood for drive-bys; 2) Ask staff members to schedule meetings; 3) Hold court in the company cafeteria for 30 minutes each day.

8. Thou shall not check your email more than twice daily.
Many of my clients have told me that they feel guilty if they don't respond to the 250 emails they get every day, but get completely lost in the black hole of time management if they do. Here are a couple of tips. Check your email no more than twice a day. Respond only to those emails from top bosses or from people who will help forward your agenda.

9. Though shalt go to the office as little as possible.
Sure it is good to have a place where you can meet people without wasting time driving around, but only up to a point. A big organization with a big office, teeming with people who want your attention, is one of the biggest time wasters ever invented. Find other places to work.

10. Thou shalt find time for eating healthy and for fitness.
The first commitment you need to have is to your health and well-being. People stop in to grab a greasy hamburger or ice cream at the company cafeteria when they are pressed for time. People don't exercise for the same reasons, and both can become bad habits. The best way to avoid this is to schedule time for regular meals, as well as regular exercise. I also suggest hiring a fitness coach who you meet with weekly. Get a good massage at least once a week.

11. Go back and review your calendar each month in reverse, analyzing every scheduled activity.

Analyze and label each activity "difference maker" or "time waster"? The goal is to get at least 30 to 70 percent of your time into the "difference maker" category.

SUMMARY

- Take control of your calendar.
- Divide your day according to the Four Quadrants of Time Management, spending approximately twenty-five percent in each: *Impossible Future, Day Job, Executive Team Member, Personal Renewal*
- Focus on the most important thing you can do *today* in each category (the epicenter for that activity) and *do it.*
- To find the most leveraged actions to take regarding your Impossible Future, stand in the future and think back to find the missing pieces that you must put into place to achieve your Impossible Future.
- Look at your calendar for the past month and distinguish between what you have done that "makes a difference", that was "important" and those activities that were merely "trivial".
- Ask yourself: *What activities that "make a difference" can you do more or; what "important" things can you do less of or delegate; what do you have to do to get the "trivial" off your calendar?*

CHAPTER 10

TRACK ACCOMPLISHMENTS: HOW AM I DOING?

Focus on the Scoreboard

IT'S IMPORTANT TO take stock of how you are doing with your 100 Day Plan, based on your own assessment and comments solicited from others. At the core, what you want to find out is how you are doing with preparing for an Impossible Future, as well as how you are doing with keeping your Day Job. I can't overemphasize how critical it is to seek feedback in both of these areas. It is totally possible to score as many goals as Pelé with respect to your Impossible Future in your first 100 days, while also totally failing at your Day Job. At the same time, it is possible for you to be doing brilliantly on your Day Job even while realizing your first 100 day goals. However, if by chance you are having issues on either side of the equation, then you will want to get some early feedback so that you can put in the correction.

THE HONEYMOON MAY ALREADY BE OVER

Just as every president or prime minister goes through an initial honeymoon period after being elected, so does every new executive, and usually that period lasts only about 100 days. The honeymoon period is the time people cheer you on and want you to succeed. Even if people see you make mistakes during this period, they will usually give you the benefit of the doubt. However, as we all know, the honeymoon period is often short-lived. It's possible for both supporters and skeptics to shift from giving you the benefit of the doubt to dropping into a judgmental mode: "I don't see that Joe has a vision that will make a difference," or "Marilyn isn't doing her Day Job." Further there is always the possibility that you have flown in the face of some industry orthodoxy that is widely accepted in your organization or stepped into someone else's control ground.

Most executives get caught up in reaching for goals and driving their agenda, as well as the daily grind of back-to-back meetings. Yet in the odd moment when it's actually possible to pause and reflect, they usually have a vague, intuitive feeling about how they are doing, which they often experience with their stomachs dropping. "I feel like I am doing great with my boss Charlie, the head of marketing. He has been very encouraging with respect to my Impossible Future and he has gone out of his way to help me clear some hurdles with my Day Job. Further, other members of the executive committee are at least mildly encouraging. However, I think some of the business unit leaders are threatened by any marketing strategy driven by corporate headquarters. I have this gnawing feeling that Mike Edwards, the SVP of our biggest business unit, just doesn't like me."

ASSESS YOUR FIRST 100 DAY PLAN

It is important to assess how you are doing with both your Impossible Future and your Day Job periodically. I suggest that at the end of each 30 days, sit down and take some time to reflect on how you are doing. You can start by taking a piece of paper and on the front side write down how you are doing on your Impossible Future. On the back side write down how you are doing on your Day Job.

Now, take a look at your First 100 Day Plan for a few minutes and ask yourself the following questions, preferably with a coach or a thinking partner, to assess what you have accomplished and, just as importantly, what you have not accomplished.

Assessing Your First 100 Day Plan

- My goals for my first 100 days are…. (List 5 to 10 things you really want to achieve.)
- Which of my goals have I actually accomplished and which ones I can be proud of? (List as many items as possible.)
- Which issues and dilemmas are showing up that I need to consider before proceeding any further?
- What's missing that, if provided, would make a difference in either furthering my goals or addressing any issues and dilemmas?
- What are my next steps? (Write down a 30-day action plan that will address what's missing.)

It is Important to Note: "What's missing" is different from "what's wrong". "What's wrong" might be the fact that your boss isn't being much of an executive champion. Or you are getting some pushback from executive committee team members. Or your family life is suffering. Whereas "what's missing" is a new idea, a fresh approach, an innovative solution that will allow you to conquer breakdowns and will help you to make further progress. "What's missing" is not always obvious, so it's a good idea to brainstorm about this with a coach or a thinking partner over time.

GET FEEDBACK FROM OTHERS

It is one thing to assess your own progress, but please keep in mind that no matter how *well or badly* you think you are doing with your

Impossible Future and Day Job, we all suffer from the phenomenon of blindness. We can't see ourselves as others see us, nor can we easily detect our own errors. I would *therefore* advise *you to* proactively seek to understand people's perceptions of you—and the reasons for those perceptions—and then, if necessary, to alter them. The easiest way to do this is to create opportunities for you to breeze into people's offices and sincerely ask the question, "How I am doing?" It's amazing how easy it is to get feedback which will help you rip the blinders off.

Remember the phenomenon of blindness. We all suffer from it.

You want people recognizing that you really are capable of an Impossible Future that, if achieved, will make a difference. At the same time, you want to find out if you are doing everything necessary to hold on to your Day Job. Create the opportunity to get this feedback from some individuals and groups. For example, first and foremost you want to find out how you are doing in your boss's eyes. You also may want to get feedback from key people at the executive committee—the CFO, the VP of Marketing, VP of Production or anyone else whose thumbs-up or thumbs-down on your performance can make you or break you. You will want to get feedback from peers and direct reports.

Keep a list of the people whose feedback you think it is important to receive, and then write down their comments as you speak with them. Note any actions you feel that you need to take as a result of this feedback.

SHIFT ANY NEGATIVE CONVERSATIONS ABOUT YOUR

One of the things that we say at Masterful Coaching is that, after the first 100 days, there is usually a conversation out there in the organization with your name on it. "Joe is a great guy," "smart as a whip," "a real team player," "he has hit the ground running." Or "Joe is a jerk," "second rate intellect," "always polishing his own star, but hasn't proven himself yet." I have observed that it takes very little on an executive's part to generate such conversations, whereas shifting the conversation can be very challenging.

> *There's a conversation out there*
>
> *with your name on it.*

For example, the conversation, Joe is great on his Impossible Future, but he is neglecting his Day Job is not a conversation you want out there about you, and you need to take steps to shift that conversation. I suggest a three-part formula: 1) Acknowledge the conversation, "So you think I am neglecting my Day Job." 2) Take responsibility for the conversation: "I have been really zeroing in on my Impossible Future and creating the business. Maybe I need to strike a better balance." 3) Start to shift the conversation. Tell people, "Here is what I intend to do differently...." Alternatively, people may have jumped to conclusions about you. If you feel this is true, then I recommend that you walk them down the ladder of inference by asking: What are the reasons or data that led you to that conversation about me? Asking these questions can set the stage for dramatically altering people's perceptions of you. (See the Ladder of Inference, Diagram 10.1)[26]

Diagram 10.1 The Ladder of Inference is a tool to understanc your own and others' reasoning process.

ACTIONS *I take*

BELIEFS *I adopt*

CONCLUSIONS *I draw*

ASSUMPTIONS *I make*

MEANING *I add*

DATA *I select*

WITNESSABLE DATA

DEVELOP A LIST OF KEY PERFORMANCE INDICATORS

In many cases you will discover that people misread how you are doing with your Impossible Future or Day Job because they didn't fully understand what you were up to. It's a good idea to be prepared to tell people what your Impossible Future is and what progress you are making, particularly with your 100-day catalytic breakthrough projects. Please don't be surprised if you hear, "Wow you are really doing a lot!" It's also a good idea to create a list of key performance indicators for your Day Job and to stay on top of them as well.

Later on, this data will be a record of actual performance benchmarks, which you can potentially use to offset negative feedback if necessary. I advise picking three to five key performance indicators rather than a laundry list. As an example, for marketing you might chose the following three performance indicators: 1) number of game-changing products in pipeline, 2) sales to date, and 3) gross margins are all good key performance indicators.

ASSESS YOURSELF ON THE FIRST 100 DAY

Besides assessing how you are doing with your 100 Day Plan, it can also provide you with some very useful insights to assess yourself on how you are doing in terms of all the steps that we have put forth here for your first 100 days in this book. Spend some time look at the following questions about your first 100 days.

How Am I Doing in My First 100 Days?

1. Preparing myself to take on this job?
2. Being clear on my going in mandate: roles, goals and expectations?
3. Doing my due diligence: gaining knowledge of the external business environment and current state of business?
4. Preparing for an Impossible Future and keeping my Day Job?
5. Dealing with any immediate crisis: making good decisions and judgment calls?
6. Building a team of 'A' players—getting the right people on the team?
7. Mastering the political chessboard?
8. Launching some immediate change initiatives and getting some quick wins?
9. Managing my calendar, balancing the transformational and transactional?

After you have answered each of the questions, take a look at what is missing that, if provided, will make a difference and key actions that you can take in the next 30 days to provide that.

It's a Roller Coaster Ride

Many people who do this exercise report that they are surprised by how much they have actually accomplished. For example, the chances are that you will *realize that you have* not only formulated your Impossible Future (for example: "To create a world class brand," or "To penetrate emerging markets"), but *also* taken powerful steps in launching some 100-day catalytic breakthrough projects that will help you achieve it.

Amazingly there are a lot of indications that momentum is actually building and you might feel like you are climbing high on the roller coaster of life. However, the next minute, you might find yourself crashing. Doing the exercise not only highlights what you have accomplished, but also will highlight the issues and dilemmas that you are facing. I want to emphasize again that in either case, focus on "what's missing that, if provided, will make a difference."

OTHER'S ASSESSMENT ON YOUR FIRST 100 DAYS

Once you do your own assessment of how you are doing in your first 100 days, it is vitally important to get an assessment from other people. It is important to have the necessary openness and willingness to ask other people to assist you in holding up a mirror. Oftentimes we suffer from what psychologists call the "halo effect" of getting some early successes, thinking that we are really doing very well and have everyone's approval, when in fact, we are not doing as well as we think and we are actually turning people off. Draw up a list of key people with different views and perspectives and ask them the same questions with respect to your first 100 days that you asked yourself earlier.

Ask People: How Am I Doing With Each of the Following?

1. Preparing myself to take on this job?
2. Being clear on my going in mandate: roles, goals and expectations?
3. Doing my due diligence; gaining knowledge of external business environment and current state of business?
4. Preparing for an Impossible Future and keeping my Day Job?
5. Dealing with immediate crisis: making good decisions and judgment calls?
6. Building a team of 'A' players—getting the right people on the bus?
7. Mastering the political chessboard?
8. Launching some immediate change initiatives and getting some quick wins?
9. Managing my calendar, balancing the transformational and transactional?

USE A COACH OR TRUSTED ADVISOR AS A THINKING PARTNER

After doing the assessments, you should have a pretty good idea of where you stand. In the end, you will be left with some key issues to deal with, like: How can I better balance my focus on the Impossible Future and Day Job? How can I lead more effectively in a crisis? How can I do better at building the relationships that will help me master the political chessboard? How can I go from a mediocre team to a team of superstars? How should I deal with some of the mistakes I have made, without getting stuck in defensive behavior?

Spend some time with a coach or trusted confidante—whether it's someone in the executive team, on your own staff or a professional coach as you reflect on the questions. A coach can help you to bring out your own views and also may help you as you sort through the feedback from others. A coach can help you to take the blinders off and to see what you might not at first be able to see. You might also use the coach to gather some feedback from key players around you.

One client I was working for asked me to talk to various people in a short interview to see how he was doing. Going through the feedback, we found out that he was coming off great with his boss, but alienating some other members of the executive committee and overwhelming his team. He had acquired the nickname of "The Tornado" with his direct reports because his bold goals, quick initiatives, and proactive attitude seemed to shake things up on a daily basis. Also, he was spending a lot of time out of the office with customers and breaking the pattern of his predecessor of holding monthly staff meetings. When we looked at the feedback he received, it allowed him to understand how his behavior was on the one hand helping him achieve his goals—getting things done—and where his behavior was causing him trouble—he was losing the support of his team, which he needed not only to do his Day Job, but also to create his Impossible Future.

We were then able to come up with some actions for the next 30-days to shift people's perspective and gain their support. It was clear that if he had not asked for the feedback, he would have been in the dark as to how people saw him and not have been able to do something about it.

SUMMARY

- Every 30 days, assess how you are doing on your first 100 Day Plan.
- Look at what is missing that, if provided, will make a difference and create high leverage actions to take in the next 30 days.

- Get some feedback from key people around you on how you are doing.
- Shift any negative conversations that you encounter that are out there about you.
- Keep a list of key performance indicators which is a record of your actual performance.
- Assess yourself on your first 100 days in regard to the steps in this book.
- Ask others to assess you, using the same questions.
- Use a coach or trusted advisor as a thinking partner to reflect on assessments on how you are doing.
- Come up with a 30 day action plan based on the assessments that you have made.

IN CLOSING

There are a few key things that I would like to point out in closing that I believe will help you to succeed in your first 100 days.

Use Checklists to Balance Demands of Your Impossible Future and Your Day Job

Checklists are a great way to make sure you are able to deal with staying on top of your Impossible Future and Day Job, which for many people can be a complex undertaking. Atul Gawande, a surgeon, has written a book called *The Checklist Manifesto: How to Get Things Right.* Gawande proves his point through a steady accumulation of examples, starting with an example of how checklists helped to create an Impossible Future at Boeing. The company had staked its hopes on the B-17. In 1935, the bomber crashed on its first test flight because it proved to be too complex for the skilled test pilot to manage. The U.S. Army Air Corps responded to this by ordering planes from Douglas Aircraft instead, and Boeing nearly went bankrupt. But some test pilots believed in the B-17. They came up with a takeoff checklist to guide a pilot through all the crucial steps to get the plane airborne. Checklists in hand, pilots went on to fly the B-17 for more than 1.8 million miles without an accident. The army ultimately ordered 13,000 B-17s, giving the U.S.A. a decisive air advantage in World War II, and the pilot checklists became universal.

Gawande shows how checklists can improve outcomes in any Day Job, from flying a plane, to building a skyscraper to performing a successful operation. For example, he explains how a simple five-item checklist in the operating room can dramatically reduce hospital-acquired infections, which kill 99,000 Americans a year.

I suggest creating a checklist for your Impossible Future. Break it down into two to three major goals and milestones. Then create a checklist of those activities that, if done consistently, will help you to achieve them. Yet the real value may be gained in reducing your Day Job to some key areas of responsibility, then creating a five-item weekly or daily checklist for each key area.

Gawande points out that coming up with the right checklists for your Day Job isn't always easy. However, once you succeed, checklists can create heroes. For proof he gives the example of US Airways pilot, Captain Chesley B. Sullenberger III, who famously landed his airplane on the Hudson River in January 2009 after hitting a flock of geese near New York's LaGuardia Airport. Captain Sullenberger has been hailed worldwide for the seemingly miraculous landing. But according to Gawande, Sullenberger and his co-pilot simply—yet expertly—followed a detailed emergency checklist, thereby vastly multiplying their chances of success. The experienced crew later unanimously acknowledged that it had required teamwork, preparation, and discipline to bring the plane down safely. [27]

Keep Your Organization Pointed Toward "True North"

In June of 2010 when Akio Toyota became CEO of the company his grandfather had started, he decided on an Impossible Future in his first hundred days: to make Toyota the number one carmaker on the planet and to surpass General Motors and Ford in sales. Unfortunately, he forgot his Day Job.

One of the reasons Toyota had been able to steal a good chunk of the US auto market was that Toyoda's grandfather had always kept his company pointed toward True North — which for him was "delivering high quality automobiles that could go a decade or more without ever spending an hour in the repair shop".

While you have to admire Mr. Toyoda's gumption in setting an Impossible Future of making the company the number one automaker in the world, he forgot one basic notion, and that is that Toyota is a company that lives by quality and will die by quality. Turning the company's fortunes around depends on living into its Impossible Future, while at the same time keeping the company pointed toward "True North."

"True North" refers to the governing values that shape the organization—culture, innovation, quality, service, and so on. If you talk to people at great organizations, like Proctor & Gamble, Johnson & Johnson, or IBM, they will usually tell you it is these governing values that "got us here." Yet as we see with the Toyota story, when a new leader comes in with ambitious goals, governing values can be forgotten. Don't let that happen to you.

Embrace the Enemy

The chances are that, if you are really up to an Impossible Future and seeking to bring about transformational change, you are going to create some supporters and some opposers. In fact, if you have been making any waves at all in driving your agenda, the chances are that you might even have one or two enemies.

For example, I was coaching a client who worked for a big defense contractor on a marketing initiative called "Smart Power". The idea was that the company become a proponent of "Smart Power," which would mean combining the "hard power" side of their business (things that go boom) with "soft power," which would involve doing more to build societies—like providing clean water, electrical power, schools, and so on to under-developed nations where trouble may brew.

My client had done a good job of aligning the CEO with her big idea, as well as others in the executive committee, but she had one key detractor (let's call him Rick) who was a hard-headed ex-Vietnam Vet and the number two guy in one of the major business units. He went on a nonstop negative PR campaign against my client and her idea, saying she was just trying to polish her own star. He just hated the idea of "Smart Power," visibly turning red and bristling whenever the term was mentioned at meetings. He basically thought my client was trying to take the company away from its traditional hard power business, which would have a negative impact on its reputation and profits.

Rick was known as a bit of an extremist by the CEO and others, nonetheless he had very strong opinions, and he put a lot of emotional torque into them. Even though people first discounted what he said, his words became like the worm inside the apple that slowly ate away at my client's standing, and the soft pulp of her idea. She made the mistake that many leaders make when they feel under attack, which is to privately criticize and publically avoid the person they see as the enemy. Her words were "no one listens to him anyway." The long and the short of it was that she avoided him for months which only seemed to empower him.

One day I sat down with my client and talked to her about a concept I use in my work called "embrace the enemy." It means instead of hiding from your enemy and rejecting their ideas, come out of hiding and engage them in a conversation with the intention of what the I Ching calls "working on what has been spoiled." Just sitting down with the person face-to-face can make a human connection, regardless of your disagreement and can often heal a lot of bruised feelings. Always keep in mind that you don't have to be disagreeable in order to disagree.

Another key part of embracing the enemy is to recognize that there are many sides of the truth to consider. In a nutshell, things go awry when you treat other people's truth as the enemy. The way to turn enemies into friends is to stop treating other people's truth as the enemy. This requires listening, building common ground, and the willingness to be influenced.

Keep Up the Momentum

An Impossible Future is not a goal. An Impossible Future is an imagined future that is very robust. The key to realizing it is to "live into that future" by making sure all of your speaking, listening, and actions are consistent with it. It means that you keep doing the thing that will get you from here to there, taking obstacles in stride because there are bound to be some.

When people are excited about an Impossible Future, whether in business or in their personal life, they usually start out with a lot of drive, with their foot pressed against the accelerator. In many cases, they actually achieve some quick wins or impressive results. Sometimes they get so impressed with themselves that they get out of the car or take their foot off the accelerator and slow down. "Oh I think I will get back to my Day Job." Yet sooner or later, they realize they have not done anything on their Impossible Future in months.

The other version is that in seeking to realize their Impossible Future and maybe scoring some early successes, they hit some obstacles. "Oh I didn't know this was going to be so difficult." At this point, a lot of people just plain give up, while deceiving themselves and others that they are still going for it. "I will get back to that soon, but first…" Maybe they are afraid of how tall the mountain is they have to climb or maybe they are intimidated by the political fallout from the journey.

My advice to you at this point is to continue to live into your Impossible Future. Your job as a leader is to speak, listen, and take action in the direction of your goals. So whether you have achieved some positive momentum already or not, please don't ever let up. The same goes for hitting obstacles, whether budgetary or political. Just don't let up!

* * *

As you take your first 100 days journey, I would love to hear from you about the obstacles you have met, the issues and dilemmas you have faced and overcome, and the Impossible Futures that you have created. I would also like to hear from you if you are just starting out and want a "Watson to your Sherlock," a thinking partner as you take the trek through your first 100 days. If I can be of service to you in anyway, please feel free to reach out at Robert.Hargrove@rhargrove.com. Good luck on your journey!

ACKNOWLEDGEMENTS

There are some people who I would like to acknowledge in this book who have either inspired me with their ideas on the first 100 days or supplied me with practical know-how. While there are actually many people, in the interest of brevity, I will focus on those who had the most profound influence.

The first is James MacGregor Burns, the noted presidential historian who I met at a Renaissance Conference and there after struck up a relationship. His books on FDR's first 100 days and thoughts on *transformational leadership* are absolutely brilliant. I realized from him that leaders not only must have big dreams, but must master the vagaries of the political chessboard to realize them.

I would like to acknowledge Dr. Edward Choi, friend and partner, for his inspiration in telling me "Dr. Hargrove, you should be coaching presidents in their first 100 days." This caused me to reframe not just my own personal and organization ambitions, but also the way I was looking at the book. This book has been written for presidents, ministers, CEOs, and executives of every ilk. Though I may use a government example here or a business example there, if you read them extrapolatively, you can translate them to your situation.

I also would like to acknowledge a good friend and former client, Greg J. Goff, CEO of Tesoro (125 on the list of the Fortune 500). The way he talked to me about his first 100 days, also reframed the whole way I was looking at the topic. The first 100 days is not just for presidents who want to make history, but for **CEOs** who need to make money for their shareholders. Greg provided a blueprint for taking a struggling business that is bleeding cash, and turning it around so that it becomes highly profitable before the first 100 days is up, and then setting the stage for accelerated growth. I relished our conversations about this!

I would also like to acknowledge that to some degree I stand on the shoulders of others who have authored books on this subject of both a practical nature. Most notably Michael Watkins, *The First 90 Days*, and Thomas J. Neff and James M. Citrin's book. *You're in Charge, Now What?* What I tried to do in *Your First Hundred Days: Powerful First Steps on the Path to Greatness* was to contribute a missing piece, which the subtitle emphasizes.

Finally, I would like to acknowledge Susan Youngquist, who acted as my publisher, editor, and graphic designer during the course of this project. If it were not for her unrelenting support and tireless, painstaking efforts, this book would never have come to pass.

Robert Hargrove

ABOUT THE AUTHOR

Robert Hargrove is one of the world's great thought leaders on executive coaching and has the motto "Better leaders; Better world." According to Robert, "Leadership is about making a difference, and if it isn't, it becomes merely a management technique."

Robert has played a huge role in making coaching a distinct profession and distinct practice with the over 100,000 coaches in the world today, the majority of which have been profoundly influenced by his methods. Robert's book *Masterful Coaching*, now in its third edition, put a stake in the ground that distinguished coaching—which is about creating Impossible Futures and bringing about transformational change in individuals and organizations—from psychology which is about resolving the past and transactional change (shifting attitudes and behaviors).

Robert is the former director of the Harvard Leadership Research Project and has been involved in coaching many top executives in business and government in their first 100 days, a time that is pivotal to any leader's success or failure. His clients have risen to positions such as the Under Secretary of Defense, the President of the New York Stock Exchange, and the European CEO of the year. Robert has been called a "great scholar," a "great writer," and a "mountain mover" when it comes to catalyzing organizational change.

Yet Robert personally prides himself on being a classic entrepreneur, the kind that seeks to dominate his industry or create a new niche. Besides being the chairman of Masterful Coaching, *world leader in executive coaching*, he and his colleagues have helped other business leaders add over five billion in profitable revenue.

He has helped new CEOs in their first 100 days take companies through all phases of business evolution: 1) start up, 2) turnaround, 3) accelerated growth, 4) reinvention, and 5) sustaining success.

Asked what he would like his legacy to be, Robert replied, "All human beings have an innate capacity for leadership. I would like my legacy to be bringing out this innate capacity for leadership so as to help people at all levels to make a difference in their world."

You may contact Robert at Robert.Hargrove@RHargrove.com.

Endnotes

1   "Pepsi: Repairing a Poisoned Reputation in India", *Bloomberg Businessweek*, June

2   Thomas Neff and James Citrin, *You're In Charge, Now What?* (Crown Business, March 2007)

3   Mehdi Hasan, "How Dave hit the ground sprinting," *New Statesman*, August 9, 2010 www.faqs.org/periodicals/201008/211471981.html

4   "QA with Jeff Immelt," *Bloomberg Businessweek*, September 17, 2001

5   Mehdi Hasan, "How Dave hit the ground sprinting," *New Statesman*, August 9, 2010

6   ibid

7   Submitted by New Deal Democrat, "The Great Depression, Part 2", *The Economic Populist*, Wed. January, 7, 2009

8   Arthur Schlesinger, Jr. commentary "The 'Hundred Days' of F.D.R.", *New York Times*, April 1983

9   Thanks to conversations with historian and renowned author, James MacGregor Burns.

10 Thomas Neff, James Citrin, *You're in Charge—Now What?*, (Crown Business, 2005)

11 ibid

12 *Scan, Focus, Act* model was first introduced by the Meta Systems Group in 1983, and developed further by Matt and Gail Taylor into conversational process

13 Mike Musgrove, "New AOL Chief to Staff: Think Bigger," *The Washington Post*, 01/17/2009

14 Video on Mindset of the CEO, Paul Drechsler on the First 100 Days, http://www.mindsetoftheceo.com/videopage.aspx?v=02913267-534f-412f-be45-1f99b2a2fd6e

15 Corner Office, condensed by Adam Bryant, "Filling In and Rising to the Tip", *New York Times*, September 20, 2009

16 ibid

17 David Magee, *Jeff Immelt and the New GE Way*, (McGraw Hill, March 9, 2009)

18 Where Leadership Starts, by RA Eckert, www.icti.ie/articles/Where%20Leadership%20Starts.pdf

19 I am especially appreciative of conversations with Greg Goff, former coachee and friend.

20 Larry Bossidy and Ram Charan, *Confronting Reality: Doing What Matters to Get Things Right*, (Crown Business, October 19, 2004)

21 I want to thank John Young, friend and former client, for this story

22 James McGregor Burns, *Running Alone: Presidential Leadership from JFK to Bush II—Why It Has Failed and How We Can Fix It*, (Basic Books, September 1, 2005

23 Judith Martin and Conrad Schmidt, "How to Keep Your Top Talent," *Harvard Busine8ss Review,* May, 1010

24 Robert Schaffer, *The Breakthrough Strategy*, (Harper Perennial, January, 1990)

25 Jason Fried and David Hansson, *Rework*, (Crown Business, 2010)

26 Ladder of Inference was developed by Chris Argyris of Harvard University. See *Knowledge for Action*, (Jossey-Bass)

27 Atul Gawande, *The Checklist Manifesto: How to Get Things Right*, (Picadore, 2011)

Made in the USA
Lexington, KY
30 December 2013